# Dining with the Durrells

# *About the author*

**David Shimwell** graduated from Durham University with degrees in botany and vegetation ecology and has had a life-long career researching and lecturing in botant, biogeography and environmental conservation. He has made a study of the Durrell family one of his lifelong passions. As an ecologist and *bon viveur*, he has designed and led many expeditions to Corfu to find the 'essence' of the Durrells through remaining family, friends and the enchanting places they knew so well. As a botanist, his special interest has been the identification and cataloguing of the wild plants in the island used for culinary purposes and in folk medicine.

# Dining with the Durrells

## Recipes from the Indian & Corfiot Cookery
### Archive of Mrs Louisa Durrell

## DAVID SHIMWELL

**HODDER &
STOUGHTON**

First published in Great Britain in 2019 by Hodder & Stoughton
An Hachette UK company

I

Copyright © David Shimwell 2019

The right of David Shimwell to be identified as
the Author of the Work has been asserted by him in
accordance with the Copyright, Designs and Patents Act 1988.

A CIP catalogue record for this title is available from the British Library

Hardback ISBN 9781529337532
eBook ISBN 9781529337549

Typeset in Bembo MT Pro by
Palimpsest Book Production Ltd, Falkirk, Stirlingshire

Printed and bound by Clays Ltd, Elcograf S.p.A.

Hodder & Stoughton policy is to use papers that are natural, renewable
and recyclable products and made from wood grown in sustainable forests.
The logging and manufacturing processes are expected to conform
to the environmental regulations of the country of origin.

Hodder & Stoughton Ltd
Carmelite House
50 Victoria Embankment
London EC4Y 0DZ

www.hodder.co.uk

*For Sal*

# Contents

Mother Louisa Durrell with Gerry and Leslie.
Bournemouth, Spring 1935.

# Foreword by Lee Durrell

The assembly, preparation and consumption of meals, from sumptuous feasts to simple fare, were a preoccupation of the Durrell family for over two generations. I was lucky enough to experience what mother handed down to son and am delighted that my wonderful friend, David Shimwell, has described the tradition so enchantingly in this book.

Gerry immortalised his family (and some of the meals they shared) in books, short stories and articles about his childhood in Corfu in the 1930s. David weaves bits of all of these into his tale, as well as prose from Gerry's brother, Lawrence, and from his mentor, Dr Theodore Stephanides. But the centrepiece is the collection of recipes from Louisa Durrell, innocent and artless matriarch of the family, who nevertheless was its lynchpin.

Very sadly, I never met Louisa, as Gerry and I married fifteen years after she passed away. Nor did I meet brother Leslie, but I came to know Larry and sister Margo very well and had the great privilege of meeting Theodore on several occasions. During my time, Larry would eat frugally and Marg sparingly, while Theodore would show me his microscope slides, including those containing the contents of the 'Pond Life Sandwich'.

Reading David's book, however, has unexpectedly brought me closer to my mother-in-law, for much of what Gerry and

I shared clearly harked back to Louisa. Many of the words and phrases David uses to describe her dishes and parties conjure up my own vivid images of life with Gerry, from hosting lively gatherings on balmy summer afternoons in Mediterranean climes to tucking into tea and scones suffused with cream and jam at the Ritz. We would serve *taramasalata* and *skordalia* as appetisers and take hours over making the 'small, small tings' to complement cauldrons of chicken curry (never omitting the crucial ingredients of coconut milk and hard-boiled eggs), all of which elicited enthusiastic noises from appreciative guests. Any curry left over (not likely!) would be used to make 'curry puffs' the next day.

A particularly memorable occasion was the party and meal we concocted for one of my birthdays down at Mas Michel – the Mazet – in the 1980s. The Mazet was the old farmhouse near Nîmes where Larry had written most of *The Alexandria Quartet* and which he sold to Gerry in 1982. It was our bolt-hole from Jersey and the trials and tribulations of trying to save the planet! Our guests included Marg (still living in Bournemouth) and Larry (now living in Sommières, a nearby village), as well as an eclectic assortment of gorgeous friends – artists and poets, builders and businessmen. Gerry had been working all morning on the *pièce de résistance* – roasted quails encircling the lower elevations of a mountain of saffron rice, crowned by peeled quails' eggs, the summit dusted with paprika and parsley. Small potatoes and florets of cauliflower and broccoli were embedded in the side of the mountain and the whole was intermingled with sultanas, almonds and pine nuts, lightly bound with cream.

He carried out the enormous platter from the kitchen toward the big table under the pergola shaded by 'grandfather's beard', treading carefully and slowly over the uneven stones of the terrace in his habitual soft moccasins, the rice mountain juddering slightly. One false step on this terrace laid by Larry twenty-five years ago . . . our guests held their collective breath . . . and erupted in cheers when he made it to the table! What can I say? The meal was worthy of . . . Louisa!

Finally, I would like to recount briefly my recent visit to Gerry's birthplace in Jamshedpur. I was leading a wildlife tour in India in 2017, but to be honest, the real reason I wanted to do this was to go to Jamshedpur and see the constructions masterminded by Lawrence Samuel Durrell, Gerry's father, for Tata Iron & Steel Company, including Beldih House, the modest bungalow where Gerry was born. It is now occupied by the charming family of a senior Tata employee, who served tea and biscuits on the lawn on the day of our visit, and invited us into the cool of the house to escape the excruciating heat. On the lawn and in the house my mind was on Louisa and her indispensable role in the Durrell story. She had been exactly here, cooking and entertaining, with the toddler Gerald at her side, perhaps too young to learn, but at the right age for absorbing scents, tastes, colours, sounds and feelings. These would surface throughout the rest of his life and add immeasurably to his writings and the influence they have had all over the world.

**Lee Durrell, October 2018**

Fiftieth Birthday Portrait of Louisa. Corfu, January 1936.

# I

# An Indian Culinary Heritage:
# Louisa Dixie-Durrell and her Cuisine

Wedding of Louisa Florence Dixie and Lawrence Samuel Durrell.
Roorkee, November 1910.

*middle row left to right*: Georgina Dixie/Lawrence Samuel Durrell/
Louisa Florence Dixie/Dora Maria Durrell ('Big Granny').
*back row left to right*: George Dixie (younger brother)/
John Dixie (elder brother)/John's wife/Samuel Amos Durrell.
*front row*: two of Lawrence Samuel's sisters,
one being Prudence (Aunt Prue)

Louisa's father, George Dixie, had died in 1907
and she was given away by her favourite brother, John.

## A Word in Advance

Let us begin the story in the summer of 1935 when the Durrell family had become established in the Strawberry-Pink Villa in the village of Perama, some three kilometres to the south of Corfu Town. Larry, the eldest son, was 23 and had begun to work on his latest piece of literary genius; Leslie was 19 and in the process of testing his collection of revolvers; at 18, Margo had taken to sunbathing in the olive groves, attired in a very skimpy swimsuit; and Gerry, being of the tender and impressionable age of 10, was discovering the entomological delights of the garden and its surrounds, a country he had labelled a miniature Lilliput. Then there was Louisa Durrell, the mother of the four siblings who could never remember the date of her birth and always insisted that it should be pointed out to anyone who might enquire that she was a widow, for as she so penetratingly observed, you never knew what people might think. She had her own special interests to help her come to terms with her new surroundings.

In between keeping a watchful eye on us all, Mother was settling down in her own way. The house was redolent with the scents of herbs and the sharp tang of garlic and onions, and the kitchen was full of a bubbling selection of pots, among which she moved, spectacles askew, muttering to herself. On the table was a tottering pile of books which she consulted from time to time. When she could drag herself away from the kitchen, she would drift happily about the garden, reluctantly pruning and cutting, enthusiastically weeding and planting.

She had steered her family through an unsettled and nomadic existence over the past seven years since her husband's death of a cerebral haemorrhage in the hill station sanatorium of Dalhousie in the mountains of Himachal Pradesh, India, on 16 April 1928, aged 43. After his burial in the British Cemetery there, she had sold the bungalow in Jamshedpur and moved the family to England, to live in the eight-bedroomed house at Dulwich, a property her husband had purchased in the summer of 1926. She was destined never to return to India, the country of her birth. The house soon proved to be far too large and its management and upkeep a drain on her financial resources, so Louisa sold it at the end of 1929, moving to rooms in the annex of the Queen's Hotel in the London suburb of Upper Norwood. Two years later, she moved her family out of the London suburbs in 1931 when she purchased a house in the village of Parkstone, five kilometres west of the southern English coastal town of Bournemouth. It was apparently here that the decision to move to Corfu was made in October 1934, after she had put the house on the market and moved the family yet again, this time into a boarding house in Bournemouth in preparation for a migration to Corfu early in 1935.

The family discussion is described in *My Family and Other Animals* in the chapter entitled 'The Migration', wherein Larry makes uncomplimentary observations on the appearance and demeanour of his mother – that she was 'looking more decrepit and hag-ridden every day'.

Mother peered over the top of a large volume entitled *Easy Recipes from Rajputana*.

'Indeed, I'm not,' she said indignantly.

'You are,' Larry insisted; 'you're beginning to look like an Irish washerwoman . . . and your family looks like a series of illustrations from a medical encyclopaedia.'

Mother could think of no really crushing reply to this, so she contented herself with a glare before retreating once more behind her book . . .

'What we all need,' said Larry, getting into his stride again, 'is sunshine . . . a country where we can grow.'

'Yes, dear, that would be nice,' agreed Mother, not really listening.

'I had a letter from George this morning – he says Corfu's wonderful. Why don't we pack up and go to Greece?'

'Very well, dear, if you like,' said Mother unguardedly. Where Larry was concerned she was generally very careful not to commit herself.

'When?' asked Larry, rather surprised at this coopera-
tion.

Mother, perceiving that she had made a tactical error,
cautiously lowered *Easy Recipes from Rajputana*.

It seems that Louisa's preoccupation with Indian cuisine was
the clinching factor behind the decision to move to Corfu,
and it was destined to be a predominant preoccupation for
the time that she and her family spent in Corfu and for the
rest of her life. The 'tottering pile of cookbooks' referred to
in the first extract quoted above and transcribed as an
Appendix to this book, is preserved in Louisa's Cookery
Archive, at Les Augrès Manor in Jersey, a unique collection
which indicates that individual items, be they handwritten
manuscripts or printed texts, range in date from 1887 to 1962,
beginning with expressions of the cuisine of the British Raj,
augmented by later English and Greek additions, from
southern England and the Ionian island of Corfu. Alas, the
apparently influential cookbook bearing the title of *Easy
Recipes from Rajputana* is not archived; and nor is the mammoth
cookery book entitled *A Million Mouthwatering Oriental Recipes*
which Louisa allegedly received in her mail in the second
paragraph of 'The Merriment of Friendship', the final chapter
in *The Garden of the Gods*. It seems that neither title ever
existed and that both were figments of Gerry's artistic licence.

Let us present a context for Louisa's culinary and entertainment skills from the descriptions of her spectacular parties
in Corfu. In Chapter 6, 'The Royal Occasion', in *The Garden*

*of the Gods*, when King George II of Greece paid a brief visit to the island, Gerry quoted his mother's immediate reaction: 'There'll be all sorts of parties and things, I suppose . . . When we were in India we always had parties during the durbar.' She referred to the frequent public receptions given by an Indian prince, a British regional governor, or the viceroy for a visiting monarch. The Durrell family did not throw a party for the Greek king, but they did present their own version of a durbar later in the year and they actually employed the king's butler from the palace at Mon Repos. Gerry begins Chapter 8, 'The Merriment of Friendship' with: 'It was towards the end of summer that we held what came to be known as our Indian party.' This last chapter in *The Corfu Trilogy* is sheer delight and the description of the fare a sub-limation of Louisa's culinary art.

> At last everything was ready. The sliding doors between the dining room and drawing room had been pulled back and the vast room thus formed was a riot of flowers, balloons and paintings, the long tables with their frost-white cloths sparkling with silver, the side tables groaning under the weight of the cold dishes. A suckling pig, brown and polished as a mummy, with an orange in his mouth, lay beside a haunch of wild boar, sticky with wine and honey marinade, thick with pearls of garlic and the round seeds of coriander; a bank of biscuit-brown chickens and young turkeys was interspersed with wild duck stuffed with wild rice, almonds and sultanas, and

woodcock skewered on lengths of bamboo; mounds of saffron rice, yellow as a summer moon, were treasure-troves that made one feel like an archaeologist, so thickly were they encrusted with fragile pink strips of octopus, toasted almonds and walnuts, tiny green grapes, carunculated hunks of ginger and pine seeds. The *kefalia* I had brought from the lake were now browned and charcoal blistered, gleaming in a coating of oil and lemon juice, spattered with jade-green flecks of fennel; they lay in ranks on the huge plates, looking like a flotilla of strange boats tied up in harbour.

Interspersed with all this were plates of small things – crystallized orange and lemon rind, sweet corn, flat thin oat cakes gleaming with diamonds of sea salt; chutney and pickles in a dozen colours and smells and tastes to tantalize and sooth the taste buds. Here was the peak of culinary art – here a hundred strange roots and seeds had given up their sweet essence; vegetables and fruits had sacrificed their rinds and flesh to wash the fowl and the fish in layers of delicately scented gravies and marinades. The stomach twitched at this bank of edible colour and smell . . .

Perhaps the most important feature of Louisa Durrell's life in India was her breadth of geographical experience of the subcontinent and the differences in its regional cuisines. The nature of her father's job in navigation engineering and husband's job as a railway engineer imparted to her a unique experience of India in the late nineteenth and early twentieth centuries, and a breadth of understanding of the country greater than most other women of her generation. Let us look closer at the nature of these experiences.

## The Dixies of Roorkee and the Military Durrells

Mother Durrell as referred to in *The Corfu Trilogy* was born Louisa Florence Dixie in the town of Roorkee (Rourki), in the North-West Provinces of northern India on 16 January 1886, the daughter of Irish Protestant parents. In the Durrell Archives at Les Augrès Manor, Jersey, there is a partial genealogy of the first three generations of the Dixie family to suggest its origin with Louisa's grandfather, John Dixie (1819–1856), who had emigrated to Delhi during the ravages of the Irish Potato Famine (Great Hunger), 1845–52. It was there that he married Johanna Doherty and in 1847, took a job as a navigation engineer for the East India Company on its major Upper Ganges Canal Irrigation project at Roorkee where the family was destined to put down its roots.

One of the main obstacles of the Upper Ganges Irrigation Project was centred in the vicinity of the town of Roorkee where the fall of the river was so sharp that it necessitated the construction of an aqueduct to carry the water downstream for 500 metres. Because of its reputation as a major symbol of British dominance in the subcontinent, the engineering works at Roorkee were identified as a leading potential target during the 1857 Indian Rebellion (Mutiny), in spite of the fact that the town was from 1853 – and remains until today – the headquarters of the regiment known as the Bengal Sappers. The town was on high alert and there is a strong Durrell family tradition, alluded to by Lawrence in his memoirs, that grandmother Johanna Dixie sat on the veranda of her bungalow with a loaded rifle on her lap, protecting her three children, Charlotte (11), Mary Ann (7) and George (2), the latter destined to become the father of Louisa.

Louisa's father, George Dixie (1855–1907), received a good education and his career prospered as the grand irrigation scheme, initially sponsored by the East India Company, was taken over by the administration of the British Empire and eventually grew to irrigate 767,000 acres in 5000 villages. It was in Roorkee that the Thomason College of Civil Engineering was founded in 1847 and the Canal Workshop and Foundry established in 1852. George progressed to become head clerk and accountant of the Ganges Canal Foundry in the town, clearly a position of elevated status in the middle stratum of society of the British Raj. In 1881, he married Georgina Nimmo Boustred and the marriage yielded three sons and one daughter. It was here that Louisa met her husband-to-be, Lawrence Samuel Durrell, a young railway engineer who had learned the practical experience of his trade working for the North-West Railway in Lahore, rising to the position of overseer in 1908 at the bridge over the River Sutlej, near Jullundur (Jalandhar). To further his career through the acquisition of a professional qualification, he had enrolled at the College of Civil Engineering in Roorkee in 1909 and the following year he married Louisa. She was 24 years of age and he was two years older. What kind of a man was he and what was his family background?

The Durrell family connection with the Indian subcontinent had begun when Samuel Amos Durrell, the grandfather of the four Durrell siblings who lived in Corfu from 1935 to 1939, enlisted in the Royal Artillery (Garrison & Field Artillery), 11th Brigade (E Battery) based at Newport, Isle of Wight in 1873. By March 1874, he was en route for India to begin a military career which was destined to last for almost forty years, during which time he was to see active service in the Second Afghan War and the Boxer Rebellion in China. His Brigade and Battery were stationed in Allahabad in the North-West Provinces (now in Uttar Pradesh State) during 1875–1877 before being sent to take part in the Second Afghan War from 1878 to 1880.

In 1883 Samuel Amos Durrell married Dora Maria Johnstone (1862–1943), the daughter of a sergeant-major in the Royal Horse Brigade, in Lucknow (North-West Provinces). She was destined to become known as 'Big Granny' by her grandchildren from the 1920s onwards. When their first son, Lawrence Samuel Durrell, father of the four Corfu siblings, was born on 23 September 1884, Samuel Amos was Conductor of Ordnance at Fategarh on the River Ganges, but not for long. Major upheavals came in 1885 when Samuel Amos was appointed Conductor of Ordnance at Ishapur (Ishapore) Gun & Carriage

Factory, outside Calcutta in West Bengal, and seven years later in 1892, when the family was uprooted again, this time some 1180 miles across the breadth of India for Samuel Amos to take up a similar post as Conductor of Ordnance at Ferozepore (Firozpur), Punjab (India), probably with the 51st Sikh Regiment. It was in the Punjab that the family was to be based for the longest period of time, almost fourteen years, from 1892 to 1905, and it was here that Lawrence Samuel gained his first taste of engineering, as an apprentice in the employ of the North-West Railway in Lahore. Big Granny Dora followed her husband wherever he was based and, no doubt, built up a breadth of geographical expertise in the cuisine of the Indian subcontinent from the Punjab to Bengal.

## The Travels of a Railway Engineer and his Family

Gerald's father, Lawrence Samuel, became a railway engineer and Louisa gave birth to their four children in diverse parts of the Indian subcontinent wherever their father was employed. Lawrence George (Larry, 1912–1990) was born in Jullundur in the Indian state of Punjab when his father was working for the North-West Railway Company; Margery Ruth was born in November 1915, apparently also in Jullundur, but alas, she died in infancy of diphtheria. Father Lawrence Samuel moved across to the far eastern region to work, now Bangladesh, for the Mymensingh-Bhairab Bazar Railway

Company, which was under construction from 1912 to 1918. It was during this contract that Leslie (1917–1983) was born, in either Kishoreganj or Bhairab Bazar. Father then moved on to another contract and Margaret Isabel Mabel (Margo, 1919–2007) was born in Kurseong in the Darjeeling District when her father was Chief Engineer for the Darjeeling Himalayan Railway. The youngest, Gerald Malcolm (Gerry) was born later in Jamshedpur on 7 January in 1925.

Louisa talked enthusiastically about these times when one of Larry's friends, Prince Jeejeebhoy, came to stay. Their conversation began with a discussion of the Indian class and caste system and perspectives from the wife of a chief engineer during his travels across the subcontinent. Gerry records the details in Chapter 5, 'Fakirs and Fiestas,' in *The Garden of the Gods*:

It was Mother that Jeejee really charmed into submission, for not only did he have endless mouth-watering recipes for her to write down and a fund of folklore and ghost stories, but his visit enabled Mother to talk endlessly about India, where she had been born and bred and which she considered her real home . . .

'India must have been fascinating then,' said Jeejeebuoy, 'because, unlike most Europeans, you were part of the country.'

'Oh yes,' said Mother, 'even my grandmother was born there. When most people talked of home and meant England, when we said home we meant India.'

'You must have travelled extensively,' said Jeejee enviously. 'I suppose you've seen more of my country than I have.'

'Practically every nook and cranny,' said Mother. 'My husband being a civil engineer, of course, he had to travel. I always used to go with him. If he had to build a bridge or a railway right out in the jungle, I'd go with him and we'd camp.'

At this point the various members of the family joined the conversation and proceeded to quiz Mother about her camping experiences, poking fun at the rather exotic, 'glamping' lifestyle with three marquees, carpets and furniture, set out as bedroom, dining room and drawing room. Mother was quick to put the experience into perspective.

'It was right out in the jungle. We could hear tigers and all the servants were terrified. Once they killed a cobra under the dining table.'

In spite of her travels in diverse regions of the Indian subcontinent, the glamping did not seem to lend itself to much culinary experimentation or the acquisition of recipes for regional specialities, except perhaps, in one instance. Gerry tells of his mother falling into raptures over the receipt of a mammoth cookery book, *A Million Mouthwatering Oriental Recipes*, that had just arrived in the post. In the final chapter of *The Garden of the Gods*, 'The Merriment of Friendship', he recorded:

'Madras Marvels!' she exclaimed delightedly. 'Oh, they're lovely. I remember them, they were a favourite of your father's when we lived in Darjeeling.'

## Settling in Bengal

In 1920, father Lawrence founded his own engineering company in the vicinity of the village of Sakchi, which had been renamed in 1919 by Viscount Chelmsford, Viceroy of India from 1916 to 1921, as Jamshedpur, to mark the influence of Jamshetji Tata (1839–1904), industrialist, nationalist and philanthropist, on the creation of the new industrial boom-town. The Tata Iron & Steel Company had been founded here in 1907 by his son Dorab Tata and since the first ingot had rolled off the mill in 1912, industrial development had been almost exponential. Lawrence recognised the potential employment opportunities in the area and took the decision to change his engineering interests from railway construction to general industrial engineering construction, undertaking contractual work for the Tata Company and constructing premises for the Tinplate Company of India, Enamelled Ironware Company and the Indian Cable Company.

The middle-class Europeans, mostly British and German, and American advisors from the Pittsburgh steel industry, settled to the north of the industrial town in an area that has become known as the Beldih Triangle. Here, in 1920, the European Club was founded and here also, Durrell built a modest bungalow for his family, no doubt attempting to give them a settled existence after six itinerant years following the railways. The club is now the Beldih Club, owned by the Tata Family, and the Durrell bungalow is referred to as Beldih House, owned by JUSCO (Jamshedpur Utilities and Services Company), a Tata subsidiary, and used to house its senior executives.

Louisa settled comfortably and it was here that she concocted a special curry for her infant son, Gerry – with the help of her *dhansana* (cook) and *ayah* (nanny). She also acquired two new cookery books for the kitchen shelves, both with long and explicit titles. First, there was *The Economical Cookery Book (for India): A thoroughly practical manual of simple and dainty dishes connected with the correct method of serving them . . . French culinary terms and a Glossary of Hindustani terms with English equivalents (1920)*; but if you think that title to be long, just read the dedication for *Bengal Sweets* by Mrs J. Haldar:

Dedicated with loving sympathy to the Womanhood of Bengal whose Sweet Beauty, Sweet Charm, Sweet Devotion, Sweet Grace, Sweet Manners, Sweet Temper, Sweet Voice, often secreted behind the veil, are prominently revealed in the delicate aroma, the exquisite flavour and delightful appearance of BENGAL SWEETS, 'The Perfection of Oriental Confectionary'

## *A Note on the Recipes*

The recipes have been transcribed as written, directly from Louisa's manuscripts. There are thus, necessarily, some problems with the interpretation of the ingredients and instructions. They are, however, relatively easy to follow and the task of replacing Louisa's intuitive understanding of the practicalities of cooking the recipes should be viewed as an original and pleasurable adjunct to their enjoyment. The challenge should make the appreciation of the finished product all the more enjoyable.

# Dedicated

with loving sympathy
to the

## Womanhood of Bengal

whose

Sweet Beauty, Sweet Charm,
Sweet Devotion, Sweet Grace, Sweet Manners,
Sweet Temper, Sweet Voice,

often secreted behind the veil,
are prominently revealed in
the delicate aroma, the exquisite flavour
and
the delightful appearance
of

### BENGAL SWEETS

"The Perfection of Oriental Confectionery."

Settling in Bengal: Dedication Page of Bengal Sweets

# 2

# Heritage Recipes from the Empire of Queen Victoria

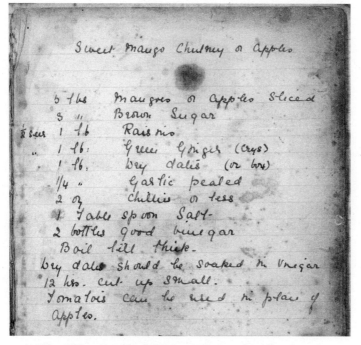

The Oldest Recipe from Louisa's Grandmother (1850s)
(Sweet Mango Chutney or Apples)

It is tempting to suggest that Georgina Dixie began to transcribe and collate the 1887 Manuscript of Recipes, the earliest collection of recipes in the Jersey Archive, primarily for her daughter, but possibly also as a commemoration of the Golden Jubilee of Queen Victoria who had been declared Empress of India in 1876. At the 1887 celebration in London on 21 June, several Indian princes were present at the ceremony in Westminster Abbey and also at the evening dinner in Buckingham Palace. A troop of Indian cavalry, formed from the 6th Prince of Wales Bengal Cavalry, marched in close proximity to the Queen's carriage in her procession through the streets of London to and from Westminster Abbey. The celebration of the Jubilee would also have been a major event in Roorkee.

It is interesting to present the constituent recipes in the 1887 manuscript and to assume that the dishes described therein were integral to the celebration of the Golden Jubilee in the North-West Provinces of India. Alternatively, the order in which they appear in the manuscript may simply be due to the random accumulation of recipes over time, whenever the mood took Georgina to write things down. It may represent some kind of popularity of foodstuff in the household, or most likely, some priority for the royal celebration. Whichever, the list is noteworthy for the predominance of cake recipes, eight described as such, and a further three related sweetmeats. A second feature is the cosmopolitan nature of the recipes, typical of an Anglo-Indian kitchen in Victorian times and taken as being of importance in the cuisine of the British Raj. By name there are Yorkshire Pudding, Madeira Cake, German Puffs, Geneva Pasties and Jew Pickle. The only recipes seemingly of a truly Indian origin are chappatis, and the three chutneys (or 'chutnees'). The full contents list of the document reads:

Contents page: Milk Punch; Common Seed Cake; Fritters; Tap Sauce; Breakfast Cake; Soda Cake; Sponge Biscuits; Ginger Cake; Yorkshire Pudding; Madira [*sic*] Cake; Almond Cakes; German Puffs; Scones; Geneva Pasti; Sponge Cake; Mango Chutnee; Tomato Sauce; Cheese Pudding; Jew Pickle; Toffy (sic); Sweet Chutnee; A Cake; Apricot Chutnee; Chappatis

## *A Celebratory Milk Punch from 1887*

One of the immediate problems with the interpretation of the recipes is the fact that the quantities of most of the ingredients are expressed in the traditional Indian measurements. Here is a table of equivalents of Indian and Imperial measures for your interpretation. We have transcribed the details of selected 1887 recipes only in the Indian measures as a primary conversion challenge before you begin to attempt their reproduction. We have also published the recipes as written, some of which do not necessarily contain all the procedural steps and stages of concoction. Here is the first recipe in the 1887 manuscript, the only one for a drink. We hope its concoction will heighten enjoyment of the rest of the book! *Saubhaagy!*

1 *seer* (sr) = 2 pounds (lbs)
1 *chittak* (cht) = 2 ounces (oz)
1 *kachcha* (kach) = ½ an ounce
1 *tola* = 180 grams (g)
1 *anna* = 11¼ grams
4 *kachcha* = 1 *chittak* = 5 *tolas* = 2 ounces

## Milk Punch

Some prefatory notes are needed. A *digchie* or *degchi* is a brass or copper cooking pot with a narrow neck and round bottom; a *seer* is an Indian measure the equivalent of two pounds; the Hindi spelling for lychee is *leechee*, here phonetically spelled as 'laichee'; a jelly bag is a fine-mesh strainer of either muslin or cheesecloth.

Take the skins of 13 limes soused in one bottle of rum for two days. Put 3½ lbs of sugar in a large *digchie* and on that pour a bottle of lime juice; pour in 3½ bottles of boiling water – pour it backward and forward for 20 minutes, then add the rum one bottle at a time, still continuing the pressing operation. Add the lime peel & the rum then add three pints or 1½ *seers* of boiling milk, stir round twice & let it stand covered up for 8 hours. Strain through a jelly bag. When boiling the milk put these spices in, 1 grated nutmeg, 12 cloves, 6 laiches, 3 black laiches, 2 sticks of cinnamon.

The phrase 'then add the rum one bottle at a time' is most perplexing, for nowhere is the number of bottles of rum specified. Also perplexing is the lack of a quantity for the milk, which one interpretation alleges is only to disguise the colour of the rum. The 1887 recipe, however, is not the only one for Milk Punch in the Durrell archives. There is an alternative in *The Economical Cookery Book (for India): A thoroughly practical manual of simple and dainty dishes connected with the correct method of serving them* (1920), recipe no. 666, which recommends the use of fifty *kagzi* limes and ten bottles of Triple X Rosa Rum (by Carew & Co., based in Uttar Pradesh), the whole to be strained through a new double flannel. Simple, maybe, but dainty, certainly not! Old Monk Triple X Rum had been manufactured by Mohan-Meakin in Ghaziabad near Delhi since 1855 and is still widely available.

There does not seem to be any reference whatsoever to the recipe for Milk Punch in any of the books of *The Corfu Trilogy*, not even as a celebratory bowl at any of the lavish durbar-style parties thrown annually by the family. Nor does the hearty beverage appear in other books by Gerry, and apparently none by Larry. Louisa may have deemed it unsuitable for her family, or more likely, have found the ingredients too difficult to obtain in Corfu, not even through the readily available resourcefulness of local friend and entrepreneur, Spiro. It is not mentioned as a substitute for the pure rum of that lewd old sea dog, Captain Creech. Perhaps it was the availability of truly Indian rum and/or fresh lychees which were the key factors responsible for its absence?

## Common Seed Cake and Other Imperial Symbols

Seed cake was one of the most traditional cakes in Britain from the time of Elizabeth I and was a popular, ever-present item at Victorian tea tables where its flavour was dominated by the seeds of caraway (*Carum carvi*) of the carrot family. If ever there was a symbol of the British Empire, it was seed cake. It was taken to the Ionian Islands when they were a nineteenth-century British protectorate where it became popular and could be still found in select Corfiot households in the 1930s. For example, when Larry and Nancy were taken to visit the former Venetian lookout overlooking the harbour of Kouloura, its owner Madame Gennatas, an old Greek lady, served tea and provided many anecdotes of the island she had known as a child. The event is mentioned by Nancy's daughter, Joanna Hodgkin, in *Amateurs in Eden*.

Nancy described Madame Gennatas as 'a stony-faced, chunky old woman' who lived alone in a beautiful old house which had once been a Venetian lookout. She spoke excellent English, though the origin of her Liverpudlian accent was a mystery; her guests were served an old-fashioned tea with seed cake and goats' milk (no cows in the rocky north of the island).

## Common Seed Cake

*4 cht /8oz unbleached flour*
*4 cht /8oz cracked wheat flour*
*3 cht /6oz sugar*
*4 cht /8oz (½ gill) milk*
*2 cht /4oz butter*
*1 cht /2oz (½ gill) warm ale*
*2 eggs beaten*
*good pinch of salt*
*1 kach /½ oz dry yeast*
*½ cht /1oz crushed caraway seed*

Sift flours and salt into large bowl. Dissolve yeast in warm ale with small amount flour mixture. Cream butter and sugar together then beat in eggs and spice mixture. Make a well in flour mix and fold in dissolved yeast, followed by butter-seed mixture. Slowly beat in milk to make a thick smooth batter. Pour batter into an 8 inches greased cake pan and bake in medium heat charcoal oven for three-quarters hour. Cool a little before turning out.

While the seed cake was described as being of the 'common' type, so several of the other recipes are rather plain and ordinary, such as the breakfast fare of both Fritters and Breakfast Cake. Here are their prescriptions, transcribed verbatim from the original manuscript which pays little or no mind to punctuation, spelling or grammar.

## Fritters

Plain fritters are made with water or dissolved butter, instead of milk & fried like pancakes Mix smoothly a quarter of a pound of finest flour with a pinch of salt & half a pint of water stir in one tablespoonful of dissolved butter and the yokes of three eggs. When ready to fry add the whites of the eggs beaten to the strongest possible froth finish like pancakes put sugar on

## Breakfast Cake

Take 2 lbs of flour ¼ lb of butter pounded sugar and currants a pinch of spice and salt three or 4 eggs drops of essence of lemon Put all into a basin with 3 table spoons full of brewers or patent yeast, previously mixed with a quarter of a pint of warm milk mixed into a light dough taking care to use the hands lightly when this is done put the dough into a warm place & prove for half an hour then mould it into what shapes you like when cold it must be put into a warm place for ten minutes then bake it in a moderate oven. You can put a table spoon full of carbonate of soda used if yeast is not handy & this much easier as the cake must be mixed and baked at once

Whatever the problems of interpretation with this set of recipes, whatever their representative nature, one feature stands out prominently. They are dated 1887, the year after Louisa Florence Durrell's birth. Might it thus be inferred that she was born into the art of cookery, that she was destined to have a deep, enquiring and abiding, lifelong love of the subject?

## Big Granny's Plum Pudding

Through her married life, Big Granny, alias Dora Maria Durrell, would have lived in well-appointed military accommodation of the type befitting her husband's rank as Conductor of Ordnance. She also took an interest in cooking and had the advantage of being experienced in the different cuisines of various regions of India, from West Bengal to the Punjab. Several of her recipes are to be found in Louisa's collection, often characterised by the fact that they are very large and probably collected from the canteen kitchens of the various regiments and ordnance companies to which her husband was attached, and by the addition of the word 'Indian' usually in parentheses after the name of the recipe. Thus, in the collection we find Indian Budgees, Plum Cake (Indian) and Plum Pudding (Indian Way), probably to emphasise the fact that the recipes were authentically native and not merely a product of the occupying British forces. Let us examine the recipe for the latter.

## Plum Pudding (Indian)

2lb suet put through the mincer
1lb bread crumbs
¼ lb flour
1lb brown sugar
2lb sultanas dark and light
1lb raisins
1lb mixed peel
1lb cry(stallised) ginger
2 tablespoons mixed spices
1 wine glass brandy
2 teaspoons salt
1 dozen eggs
2 tablespoons Paisley flour
1½ pints milk
½ lb butter

Mix all dry ingredients well; then rub in butter; then add eggs well beaten and the milk.

The quantities given are as written in Big Granny's recipe, therefore this produces a pudding weighing a massive twelve pounds! It seems improbable that either she or her daughter Louisa made such a large single pudding for one of her Indian parties – or even for a greedy family at Christmas lunch – rather that she made several smaller puddings, boiled in a rag in the largest utensils she possessed. Using half the amounts indicated, the pudding cooks in a pressure cooker in fifty minutes. Perhaps the size of the pudding and its cost was a characteristic reason why Granny Dora became known as Big Granny?

A copy of her manuscript recipe for Plum Pudding (Indian) is illustrated on the end page of this chapter.

## *Lost Labels: Variations on the Sweet Chutney and Pickle Theme*

Gerry's description of the fare on display at the end-of-summer Indian party in Corfu contains the phrase 'chutney and pickles in a dozen colours and smells and tastes to tantalise and soothe the taste buds.' Louisa had been collecting recipes for such fare from the time of the original 1887 manuscript, which includes recipes for three types of chutney, which Louisa invariably continued to spell as 'chutnee', in the Indian fashion, all through her time in Corfu. Here, the kitchen at Villa Anemoyanni had an important annex in the shape of a big, cool larder where Louisa stored her jars of 'chutnees', pickles and preserves and Gerry's description of the contents of this larder is most revealing, for it provides confirmation that he was aware of his mother's Indian recipe archive and that she probably produced 'chutnee' according to one or another. In a period of relative calm and quiet, she and Gerry seized the opportunity to do one of the kind of jobs she had been putting off for a protracted period of time. Gerry described the task in Chapter 5, 'Fakirs and Fiestas' in *The Garden of the Gods*.

The previous year had been an exceptionally good one for fruit and Mother had spent hours preparing various jams and chutneys, some from her grandmother's recipes from India dating back to the early eighteen hundreds. Everything went fine and the big cool larder was a-glint with battalions of bottles. Unfortunately, during a particularly savage storm in the winter, the larder roof had leaked and in consequence Mother had come down one morning and found all the labels had come off. She was faced with several hundred jars, the contents of which were difficult to identify unless you opened the jar. Now, given a moment's respite by her family, she determined to do this necessary job. Since it involved tasting, I offered to help. Between us we had got some hundred and fifty jars of preserves on the kitchen table, armed ourselves with spoons and new labels, and were just about to start on the mammoth tasting when Spiro arrived.

The above passage would seem to indicate that Louisa continued to use her grandmother Dixie's 'chutnee' recipes, which probably come from the cuisine of the North-West Provinces in the turbulent times of the late 1850s. Now would seem the time to expand this theme and discuss the necessary modifications for their concoction in Corfu. The recipes from 1887 are in a shorthand form but Louisa's recipe from the 1920s, called Sweet Mango or Apple Chutney, is much easier to follow.

## Sweet Mango or Apple Chutney

*5lbs mangoes or apples, sliced*
*3lbs brown sugar*
*1lb ½ dry raisins*
*1lb ½ dry green ginger (crystallized)*
*1lb dry dates (or box)*
*¼ lb garlic, peeled*
*2oz chillies or less*
*1 tablespoon salt*
*2 bottles good vinegar*

Boil till thick. Dry dates should be soaked in vinegar for 12 hours and cut up small. Tomatoes can be used in place of apples.

The original version of this recipe was almost certainly of Indian origin and used mangoes in preference to other fruit, India being the main producer of the fruit in the world. It is doubtful whether they would have been available in the markets of Corfu and it seems likely that Louisa's sweet Corfu chutneys would either have been based on apples or tomatoes. Another recipe from both India and Corfu was for Sweet Lime Chutney, a common citrus fruit at the peak of ripeness in January.

## Sweet Lime Chutney

Take a dozen limes, cut each into eight segments, seed and rub cut flesh with salt. Dry them in a slow oven, remove and chop coarsely. Chop together the following ingredients: ½ cup pitted dates, ½ cup raisins, 3 dried red chillies (seeded), 3 cloves garlic, ½ tbsp mustard powder, 1 cup brown sugar, 2 tbsp salt. Put chopped ingredients in a large mixing bowl and add one cup of vinegar. Add the chopped limes and stir well, leaving to stand for 30 minutes. Bring the mixture to boil, stirring occasionally, then simmer for 30 minutes. Allow to cool, then spoon the mixture into jars that have been sterilised in boiling water.

Then there were the pickles. The recipe for Jew Pickle dates from the 1887 handwritten manuscript and Louisa could also refer to recipe No. 513 in *The Economical Cookery Book*, which is substantially the same as the 1887 recipe. More correctly, it seems it should be called Jewish Pickle, but it is perplexing in that it is not a pickle made in the kosher style of brine and sugar, with no vinegar; nor does it use cucumber or gherkin as in the style of the familiar modern American kosher pickle. In some Indian/Jewish recipes, it is referred to as either Carrot Pickle or Vegetable Pickle. One theory as to why the recipe has the name of Jew Pickle is that its sweetness and the diversity of the ingredients is symbolic of a rich cuisine and lifestyle, more affluent than the Anglo-Indian cuisine. Without the vinegar, the recipe might be called Mixed Pickled Vegetables in a kosher kitchen.

The Belgian Consul, to whom Gerry did not give a personal name, was employed by his mother as a tutor to keep her son's French in trim. Spiro drove Gerry into the Jewish Quarter of town, still standing in the twenty-first century and now designated as a World Heritage Site. The scene for the pickle recipe may be set through an excerpt from Chapter 9, 'The World in a Wall' in *My Family and Other Animals*.

The consul's house was situated in the maze of narrow, smelly alleyways that made up the Jewish quarter of the town. It was a fascinating area, the cobbled streets crammed with stalls that were piled high with gaily-coloured bales of cloth, mountains of shining sweetmeats, ornaments of beaten silver, fruit, and vegetables. The streets were so narrow that you had to stand back against the wall to allow the donkeys to stagger past with their loads of merchandise. It was a rich and colourful part of the town, full of noise and bustle, the screech of bargaining women, the cluck of hens, the barking of dogs, and the wailing cry of the men carrying great trays of fresh hot loaves on their heads. Right in the very centre, in the top flat of a tall, rickety building that leant tiredly over a tiny square, lived the Belgian consul.

Today, the donkeys and the commerce may have gone and the bustle is no longer apparent, but from Albert Cohen Square, named for the Corfiot-Swiss novelist Albert Cohen (1895–1981), who coincidentally wrote in French, it is possible to look up to the top flat in the fabric of a rickety, dilapidated building where Gerry polished up his French. A visit to the Jewish Quarter is surely an essential for all international tourists; and so, perhaps, should be an appropriate pickle.

## Jew Pickle (1887)

*Half pound each of the following vegetables, cleaned and peeled: cauliflowers, carrots, peas, turnips*
*2 red chillies*
*4oz sliced ginger*
*1 teaspoonful of ground red chillies*
*1lb sugar*
*2oz salt*

Make a syrup with the sugar, salt [and a bottle of vinegar]. Add the vegetables and other ingredients and give the whole a gentle boil over a low fire. Bottle when cool.

Another popular pickle for which there is a handwritten recipe in one of Mrs Durrell's cookbooks is that for Loquat Pickle. Here are the details.

## Loquat Pickle

Peel the half-ripe fruit and sprinkle salt over them; drain after twenty-four hours. Add whole chillies to taste. Put these (the mixture) in a pan and pour in sufficient boiling vinegar to cover them. When cold, bottle and expose to the sun for a month. By absorption the vinegar gets less. More vinegar should be added and the loquats kept covered with it.

Loquats (*Eriobotrya japonica*) were apparently well known to Mrs Durrell from her Indian days and towards the end of May when the fruits were ripe, she would have been most pleased to find them growing in Corfu, where they were known as *nespoli*. Her kitchen would have been full of their scent in various stages of preparation, and from the pickling pans bubbling away on the stove. Gerry sometimes ate the fruit for breakfast and one can imagine him, already late for his lesson with his tutor, Richard Kralefsky, scooping up a handful of loquats from the kitchen table and gobbling them down as Spiro drove him into town. It seems that he was rather surprised by the loquats, because as you will observe from his mother's recipe, the fruits would have been 'half ripe'; an amusing situation arose, as described in Chapter 14, 'The Talking Flowers', in *My Family and Other Animals*.

I had worked for some weeks with Kralefsky before I discovered that he did not live alone. At intervals during the morning he would pause suddenly, in the middle of a sum or a recitation of county towns, and cock his head on one side, as if listening.

'Excuse me a moment,' he would say. 'I must go and see Mother.'

At first this rather puzzled me, for I was convinced that Kralefsky was far too old to have a mother still living. After considerable thought, I came to the conclusion that this was merely his polite way of saying that he wished to retire to the lavatory, for I realized that not everyone shared my family's lack of embarrassment when discussing this topic. It never occurred to me that, if this was so, Kralefsky closeted himself more often than any other human being I had met. One morning I had consumed for breakfast a large quantity of loquats, and they had distressing effects on me when we were in the middle of a history lesson. Since Kralefsky was so finicky about the subject of lavatories I decided that I would have to phrase my request politely, so I thought it best to adopt his own curious term. I looked him firmly in the eye and said that I would like to pay a visit to his mother.

Kralefsky was most astonished when Gerry asked if he might go and visit his mother, but nevertheless complied with his puzzling request and Gerry was eventually shown into a large shadowy bedroom, full of flowers, where the small auburn-haired figure of an old lady lay propped up in bed. She welcomed Gerry and they fell into deep conversation on the subject of whether flowers talk. Gerry immediately realised that Kralefsky's oft-used phrase 'Excuse me a moment, I must go and see mother,' was not a euphemism for saying that he wished to visit the lavatory but that, in reality, his tutor was making regular visits to check on the well-being and comfort of his bedridden parent. Gerry recounts the conversation in some detail, but nowhere does the reader discover whether he actually visited the lavatory!

Recipe for Loquat Pickle

Plum Pudding (Indian)

2 lbs Suet put through the mincer
1 " Bread Crumbs
½ lb. Flour
1 lb Brown Sugar
2 lbs Sultanas dark & light
1 lb Raisins
1 lb Mixed Peel
1 t Dry Ginger
2 Table Spoons Mixed Spices
1 Wine glass Brandy
2 Tea spoons Salt
1 doz Eggs
2 Table Spoons Paisley Flour
1½ pints milk
½ lb Butter
    Mix all dry ingredients
well then rub in butter then
add eggs well beaten & the
    milk —

Recipe for Big Granny's Indian Plum Pudding

# 3

## Curries in Context

Lawrence Samuel Durrell and Family. Jamshedpur, 1924.
(Before Gerry was born.)

It is interesting to note that none of the recipes in the 1887 manuscript are for substantial main-course dishes. One interpretation of the contents might be that the recipes collectively form a group of a Memsahib's indulgences, fancies for an afternoon's entertainment of like-minded ladies from the middle-class stratum of Anglo-Indians, or in the Dixie-Durrell case, Hiberno-Indians. We will talk more on this topic later, towards the end of this chapter. The persons charged with the everyday provision of meals were the *khansamas*, or cooks, and if there were young children in the family, the *khansamas* would often liaise with the *ayah*, the nursemaid or nanny, on the likes and dislikes of their charges. The *khansamas* were largely responsible for modification of aspects of British cuisine by the use of Indian cooking methods and the incorporation of spices, notably those unified into a variety of regional curry mixtures. Unless the Memsahib actually took an interest in the kitchen and the cuisine – as Memsahib Durrell did – many of the recipes would not become known outside the kitchen.

The versatility of Gerry's mother in the kitchen and her close liaison with her *khansamas* is clearly evident from his many descriptions in *The Corfu Trilogy*; she naturally had a meal for all occasions, to suit every type and origin of guest. But one type of cuisine gave her the greatest pleasure, namely, the culinary delights of her native country, the India of the British Raj, in particular, the intricacies of that group of dishes which are collectively referred to as 'curry.' For corroboration of this delight we should probably refer to a passage from 'At the Villa Anemoyanni' in *Autumn Gleanings* (2011), a memoir by Theodore Stephanides, a close family friend and mentor of both Gerry and Larry, himself born and nurtured in Bombay (Mumbai), with a primary taste for Indian cuisine. Theo and the family were dancing to a gramophone record of the *pendozali*, a popular Greek folk dance in which the dancers form a circle and dance with their hands on each other's shoulders.

> I showed Lawrence and the others the steps and, in next to no time, we were all dancing round and round the sitting room. It happened to be a cold grey rainy day outside so we kept this up for most of the afternoon, dancing the *pendozali* and several other Greek folk dances, the *kalamatiano*, the *syrtos* and the *trata*, which the whole Durrell family learnt with equal facility. We thus spent a very gay afternoon, in spite of the dismal weather, and worked up a wonderful appetite for supper. The latter meal almost always included a curry, as old Mrs Durrell had lived many years in India and was an excellent cook.

# *Gerry's Favourite Chicken Curry*

The recipe probably originated with Louisa, her *khansama* and Gerry's *ayah* in the kitchen of the family bungalow in Jamshedpur, where Gerry was born in 1925, now in the state of Jharkhand, but formerly in West Bengal. The original Bengali curry powder used in the recipe has a sweetness given by *amchoor* (mango powder) and *panch phoron*, a mixture of five different spices, usually a blend of the seeds of fennel, black mustard, nigella, fenugreek and cumin – the Bengali Five-Spice. The powder is mild to medium dependent on the use of chilli powder and the sweetness is further imparted by coconut milk, just to the taste of a toddler, aged 3. A mild curry powder was chosen for the 80th Anniversary version in May 2015. The use of hard-boiled eggs is adopted from the traditional Bengali Egg Curry; and finally, Louisa's influence from the cuisine of the Punjab and the irrigated lands of the North-West Province at Roorkee can perhaps be seen in the inclusion of a range of vegetables, particularly cauliflower and celery, sweet peppers and potatoes.

Here is the recipe for four persons; the specifications for the upgrade of quantities for thirty-five has been lost in the occult of time and confusion.

## Gerry's Favourite Chicken Curry

Take 2 cups chopped onions; 4 cloves garlic chopped; 3 tbsp each of butter and olive oil; 3–4 tbsp curry powder. Fry all the above slowly for at least 5 minutes, adding stock if necessary to prevent burning. Two chickens, cut into bite-size pieces, browned separately in olive oil. Make 600ml stock with half strong chicken stock and half coconut milk (tinned). Mix liquid and chicken with onion mixture. Add one roughly chopped green and one red sweet pepper and a few chopped sticks of celery. Cook on low heat and simmer for 45 minutes. Add a quantity of small potatoes and cook a further 20 minutes. Then add florets of one large cauliflower and/or chopped green vegetables (peas or beans) and cook 20 minutes more.

Hard boil eggs separately and add while warm before serving with *aloo* potatoes and/or rice.

## A Simple Curry to Combat Larry's Dyspepsia

In September 1935, Louisa and family moved from the Strawberry-Pink Villa in Perama to the much larger Villa Anemoyanni (the Daffodil-Yellow Villa) in Sotiriotissa, some six kilometres north of Corfu Town. Larry and Nancy, who had been living in a totally inadequate small box-like cottage, comprising two small rooms and a minuscule kitchen, which Larry had christened Villa Bumtrinket, moved in with the rest of the family for maybe six weeks, or two months, before they rented the White House, in the fishing village of Kalami, in the spring of 1937. Louisa and family lived in the Daffodil-Yellow Villa for two years and it was here that she revelled in the delights of experimenting with a diversity of recipes, developing the culinary skills for which she was destined to become renowned.

In spite of six months of property-hopping, Larry had been leading a predominantly sedentary life which, in retrospect, was very productive in terms of his literary output. Buoyed by the publication of his first novel, *Pied Piper of Lovers*, in 1935, he had become stimulated to write a sequel, *Panic Spring*, which was destined to see the light of day in 1937. Then, lurking in the background, coming to the fore from time to time, being picked up and set down, were passages and chapters of a manuscript written between September 1935 and December 1936, that was eventually published in 1938 as *The Black Book*. His visits to see his mother and siblings through the winter of 1935–36 were apparently frequent, but not continuous, as Gerry implies in *My Family and Other Animals*. Unfortunately, his lifestyle and the richness of his mother's cooking was beginning to have a noticeable effect on his health, as Gerry observed in Chapter 6, 'The Sweet Spring', in *My Family and Other Animals*.

When left undisturbed by Larry, however, spring for Mother meant an endless array of fresh vegetables with which to experiment, and a riot of new flowers to delight her in the garden. There streamed from the kitchen a tremendous number of new dishes, soups, stews, savouries and curries, each richer, more fragrant and more exotic than the last. Larry began to suffer from dyspepsia. Scorning the simple remedy of eating less, he procured an immense tin of bicarbonate of soda, and would solemnly take a dose after every meal.

'Why do you eat so much if it upsets you, dear?' Mother asked.

'It would be an insult to your cooking to eat less,' Larry replied unctuously.

'You're getting terribly fat,' said Margo; 'it's very bad for you.'

'Nonsense!' said Larry in alarm. 'I'm not getting fat, Mother, am I?'

'You look as though you've put on a little weight,' Mother admitted, surveying him critically.

'It's your fault,' Larry said unreasonably. 'You will keep tempting me with these aromatic delicacies. You're driving me to ulcers. I shall have to go on a diet' . . .

At the next meal he took the precaution of having a large dose of bicarbonate beforehand, and then protested bitterly that the food tasted queer.

★

48

In contrast to Gerry's childhood experience of being weaned on sweet, rich curry, Larry's basic dietary fare was much simpler, even austere, with unattractive-sounding dishes like Potato Curry, Peas and Potato Curry and Cabbage and Potato Curry. And, at times during the first year of his residence in Corfu, they were often at the forefront of his reminiscences of childhood. He must have been most gratified to see the publication of his first book, *Pied Piper of Lovers* (1935), a semi-autobiographical novel about a young Anglo-Indian boy named Walsh Clifton who is raised by his father, John Clifton, after his mother had died in childbirth. A railway engineer, Clifton takes a job in Kurseong on the northern frontier of India, to work on the narrow-gauge Darjeeling Mountain Railway, living in a rambling colonial house with a retinue of servants and an *ayah* to care for his son. Walsh becomes preoccupied with his relationship with his *ayah* and her ways, notably, for example, why she threw away her food after his shadow had fallen across it at dusk. He was roaming the garden when he found her squatting at the door of her hut about to serve steaming curry and chapattis to her husband and herself. Walsh had retreated in guilt from the angry looks of his *ayah* and her husband and later prayed that God should punish her for what he perceived as an act of superstition and gluttony.

Walsh's father introduced him to a huge, bearded Irish Jesuit priest, Father Calhoun, who was destined to become his tutor at the nearby Kurseong Monastery. Walsh made his first visit to the monastery, aged 6, when the priest invited him and his father to lunch in his private room. At a large oak table spread with a cloth, they ate a fiery potato-based curry so hot with spices that Walsh's throat was burnt and most painful due to the vast quantities of water he was forced to drink to calm his raging thirst. The fire in the dish probably came from the fiery local *khursani* chilli pepper, and its liberal use in the belief that this fire stimulated virility in young males.

Larry attended St Joseph's School, a Jesuit-run establishment at North Point in nearby Darjeeling, until the age of 11. Both Kurseong and Darjeeling were known as 'school towns' on account of the number of educational establishments located therein, many of which were run by the Jesuit Order of St Ignatius Loyola. The sparse and simple cuisine available to the boys became renowned throughout India and it is tempting to suggest that the following curry from Louisa's notes was either collected by her son from the school menu, or by herself when the family lived in the region. As you will note, the basic ingredient is potato and the embellishments are mainly peas and/or cabbage.

## Potato and Cabbage Curry (Aloo Sabzi)

Heat 3 tbsp olive oil in a pan and sizzle 1 tsp fennel seed and 1 tsp cumin seeds. Add one large sliced onion and sauté for 2 minutes. Add one large potato, peeled and cubed, and 4 cups of chopped cabbage. Mix in 1 tsp turmeric and salt to taste. Cover the pan with a lid and cook gently on slow heat for 10 minutes. Mix in 2 tsp hot chilli powder and 1 tsp garam masala and cook a further 5 minutes. Mix in a handful of fresh, chopped coriander leaves and serve.

## *Louisa's Classic Vegetable Curry*

With Larry suffering from dyspepsia, Margo on a permanent diet for her weight-watching and skin quality, Mother clearly had to take note and modify the richness and spiciness of her savoury cuisine. Perhaps she could begin with her curries; perhaps she could start by cutting out the meat and reverting to the traditional vegetable curry dishes from her youth in Roorkee.

That could have been a starting point for a programme of ensuring the better health of her children; she would cut down on the meat component of many of her meals, and it would be cheaper. In this objective, she received a helping hand from an unusual direction – through the agency of her youngest son. It all began when Gerry acquired three eagle owlets from the Rose-Beetle Man and very soon began to realise the 'culinary implications' of his new acquisitions. He began to regret that his relations with brother Leslie were slightly strained, otherwise he might have persuaded him to shoot a few sparrows, or a rat or two. The owlets were hissing, whingeing and whining as he sought out his mother, having decided that the only possible solution to satisfying his wonderful new pets was to rely on her unfailing kindness of heart. The story is told in Chapter 4, 'The Elements of Spring', in *The Garden of the Gods*.

I found her ensconced in the kitchen, stirring frantically at a huge, aromatically bubbling cauldron, frowning at a cookbook in one hand, her spectacles misty, her lips moving silently as she read. I produced my owls with the air of one who is conferring a gift of inestimable value. My mother straightened her spectacles and glanced at the three hissing, swaying balls of down . . .

She continued with her cooking, oblivious of her persistent son and his immediate problem that the owls were hungry, in fact, starving to death.

'Poor little things,' said Mother, her sympathies immediately aroused. 'Give them some bread and milk.'

I explained that owls ate meat and that I had used up the last of my meat supply. Had Mother perhaps a fragment of meat she could lend me so that the owls did not die?

'Well, I'm a bit short of meat,' said Mother. 'We're having chops for lunch. Go and see what's in the icebox.'

Gerry went to the massive icebox in the larder, spied the ten chops for lunch and decided that even these were hardly meal enough for three voracious eagle owls. He went back with the news to the kitchen.

'Oh dear,' said Mother. 'Are you sure they won't eat bread and milk?'

I was adamant. Owls would only eat meat.

At that moment, one of the babies swayed so violently he fell over and I was quick to point this out to Mother as an example of how weak they were getting.

'Well, I suppose you'd better take the chops then,' said Mother, harassed. 'We'll just have to have vegetable curry for lunch.'

After Mother had weakened and given Gerry the chops earmarked for lunch, and had served up vegetable curry instead, the uproar began, centred around Larry's diatribe against Gerry's ever-increasing menagerie, its effects on the peace and tranquillity of the household and his fears that they would all complain when their beds were waist-deep in owl vomit. His reaction might have been somewhat appeased had he realised that the owls in question were Eurasian Eagle Owls (*Bubo bubo*), an 1837 lithograph of which was destined to become one of Edward Lear's iconic illustrations in *Birds Drawn for Sir John Gould, 1832–1838*. This species was also none other than that which featured in 'The Owl and the Pussycat' rhyme, arguably the best known of Lear's *Nonsense Songs, Stories, Botany, and Alphabets* (1871). Larry's infatuation with the time Lear spent on Corfu led him to write a rather incongruous last chapter in *Prospero's Cell*, entitled 'An Anthology Drawn from the Painter's Letters.'

The family knew that Mother's Vegetable Curry was not

merely just another curry that lacked any form of meat as an ingredient, but rather, it was a special combination of vegetables and spices which originated in the North-West Provinces of India and celebrated the heritage of the Upper Ganges Irrigation Scheme in the mid-nineteenth century. Uttar Pradesh curries grew to become characterised by the use of expensive spices, such as saffron rather than turmeric, and without garam masala. Anise, bay leaves, cardamom, cinnamon, coriander, fennel seeds, garlic, ginger and nutmeg are often included in the spice mixture for the curry powder. The vegetables which usually combine in this curry are first and foremost, cauliflower, accompanied by onions, peas, green beans and split lentils, either red or green. Louisa sometimes incorporated potatoes, but her recipe was a green curry that also used spinach and sometimes the leaf vegetable amaranthus (chauli or marsa in Hindi), which was, and still is, a common garden plant/weed in Corfu.

## Mother's Vegetable Curry

*One cauliflower broken into curds*
*Two large onions, coarsely chopped*
*½ cup green lentils, soaked overnight*
*Handful green beans and/or peas*
*Large bunch spinach or spinach/amaranthus mix with coarse*
*stems removed*

*2 garlic cloves*

*1 inch ginger root or 1 tsp dry ground ginger*

*2 tsp ground coriander*

*1 tsp ground cumin*

*1 tsp turmeric or saffron for preference*

*Pinch of cayenne pepper (optional)*

*1½ cups vegetable stock*

*4 tbsp olive oil*

Heat the olive oil in a large pan on medium heat. Cook onions, cauliflower florets, green beans and green lentils until just softened. Add garlic, ginger, coriander, cumin and saffron (with optional cayenne pepper) and stir to coat the vegetables. Stir in vegetable stock and season with salt and pepper to taste. Bring mixture to the boil, cover and reduce heat. Simmer for 10 minutes to blend flavours. Stir in spinach/amaranthus leaves till they begin to wilt. Cover and simmer for 10 minutes until spinach is completely wilted and the cauliflower tender.

## *An Economical Sixpence/ 12 Drachmas Goat Curry*

Amongst the archive materials at Les Augrès Manor, Jersey, are pages 35–158 from the dog-eared and dilapidated *500*

*Cookery Dishes that You Can Make for Sixpence Each* by Mary Woodham, published in London in 1936, and describing 'Savoury and Satisfying Meals at Sixpence Each for One, Two or More People'. This slim volume, itself costing sixpence, might have been imported for the benefit of the expatriate British community in Greece, or more likely, sent directly from the London branch of the Durrell family in response to a casual comment in a letter by Louisa who had discovered that the exchange of foreign currency was a complicated process bound by strict rules. It is difficult, however, to find references to such situations of her need to set a tight budget, other than the casual, figurative suggestion by Gerry that his mother was 'always surrounded by the dangerous shoals of overdraft and extravagance'.

Louisa would have been well aware of the so-called world-wide Great Depression and would have felt some moral obligation to tighten her belt. After all, the security of her late husband's investments was not guaranteed and moreover, none of the family had a job. In addition, Greece had abandoned the international gold standard and there was uncertainty with respect to the fluctuating value of the basic Greek currency unit, the drachma, subdivided into 100 lepta. The Bank of Greece issued 50, 100, 500, 1000 and 5000 drachma notes, silver coins of 10 and 20 drachmas, cupronickel coins of 1, 2 and 5 drachmas and 20 lepta, and an aluminium 10 lepta coin. In April 1936, the average value against the pound sterling was 520 drachmas, and 107 drachmas against the US dollar, so sixpence would have been worth 12 drachmas – and by conversion to modern values, it would be worth £1.60 in 2018.

There is a sixpence/12 drachma recipe, identified by the fact that the top left-hand corner of page 138 in the *500 Recipes* book is turned down, presumably to mark the recipe for 'Mutton Curry Roll'. It might not have suited Larry's dyspepsia, but Louisa would, no doubt, have been delighted to trial it, especially on account of the fact that she could undercut the sixpence total by 1¼d, the five farthings of the 'Oranges and Lemons' rhyme, by using one of the eggs laid by her own hens. Thus, the recipe would only have cost 9 drachmas instead of nearly 12 drachmas. Also, in the copy of the recipe in the book, 'Mutton' is crossed out and 'Goat' pencilled in its place. Goat meat (chevon in English, or *bakara* in Hindi) would have been more frequently available in both India and Corfu and it is tempting to suggest that Louisa saved some cold *bakara* after a spit-roast, such as after the occasion described by Gerry in 'The Angry Barrels', the last chapter in *Birds, Beasts and Relatives*. The extended family entourage was dining on the beach below the house and vineyards of Mr Stavrodakis, in the north of the island, under the flanks of Pantokrator, where Mother and Spiro 'crouched like witches over the fires, larding the brown sizzling carcass of a kid with oil'. The Chevon Curry Roll would have been a sweet reminder of the idyllic wine harvest.

# Chevon Curry Roll

*3 tablespoonsful rice − 1d. (2 drachmas)*
*1 teaspoonful curry powder − ½d. (1 drachma)*
*1 onion − ¼d. (50 leptas)*
*Cold mutton (chevon) − 2d. (4 drachmas)*
*Chopped parsley − ¼d. (50 leptas)*
*1 egg − 1¼d. (2 drachmas 50 leptas)*
*Brown gravy, or ½ stock cube dissolved − ½d. (1 drachma)*

*Total Cost − 5¾d. (11 drachmas 50 leptas)*

Chop the onion finely and mix with the curry powder. Boil the rice in water with the onion/curry mixture until the rice is soft; drain. Chop the cold mutton remains with the parsley and mix with the cooked rice. Form the mixture into a roll, coat with flour and beaten egg and place in a buttered tin. Sprinkle with breadcrumbs and bake in a moderate oven until browned. Serve hot with brown gravy poured over.

Louisa and Gerry, 1925

# 4

# Savoury Finger Foods
# and Palate-Pleasers

Recipe for Indian Budgees

The cuisines of many cultures are well known for a collection of small appetisers, little nibbles to encourage polite informal conversations before dinner parties between guests who do not necessarily know each other well, persons who would not normally trade confidences, but who would nevertheless engage in light-hearted banter. Small plates for small talk has become a popular way of dining out in the cities of western Europe in the twenty-first century – Italian antipasti, Spanish tapas, Greek meze and Indian small plates. These small plates are, of course, based upon time-honoured traditional finger foods and palate-pleasers in each culture and, needless to say, the various members of the Durrell family indulged in the dual delights of Indian small plates. Let us delve deeper and note that the dishes are a virtual vegetarian feast.

## A Quartet of Savoury, Small-Plate Palate-Pleasers

At the start of 'The Merriment of Friendship', the final chapter in *The Garden of the Gods*, the members of the Durrell family were sitting on the veranda, planning their end-of-summer Indian party. Louisa, aka Memsahib Durrell, was entranced by the mammoth cookery book, *A Million Mouthwatering Oriental Recipes*, she had just received in the post, and kept reading out extracts to her children.

'Madras Marvels!' she exclaimed delightedly. 'Oh, they're lovely. I remember them, they were a favourite of your father's when we lived in Darjeeling.'

Madras Marvels was apparently the Durrells' colloquial name for a curried chutney canapé eaten as a relish, a finger-food appetiser before a main evening meal. The tradition of preceding a main meal with a relish to prepare the digestive tract for the subsequent feast was one which originated in the Indian subcontinent, before being spread to Europe and the New World. It comprised a cooked and pickled vegetable dish, usually in the form of chutney, often augmented by curry sauce and eaten on bread. The French popularised the practice of serving canapés as finger foods where the relish sits on top of a slice of stale bread, literally on the *canapé*, or sofa. Their production is simplicity personified.

## Madras Marvels

Cut slices of stale bread about half an inch thick, stamp with a round cutter and fry in a little butter. Fry a teaspoonful of Madras curry powder in a tablespoonful or more of butter, add a teaspoonful of mango chutney and a little salt; mix together with the yolks of two hard-boiled eggs. When cold spread evenly on the fried bread and garnish with the chopped white of egg.

Recipes for Madras curry powder and sauce vary widely in terms of their ingredients but most seem to include the five ingredients beginning with the letter 'c' – coriander and cumin seeds, cardamom pods, curry leaves and chillies – and it is probably the heavy use of the latter which gives the mixture its reputation as a fairly hot concoction. The variety of chilli used is either *bydagi* or Madras *pari*, grown in the Nellore District of Andhra Pradesh, north of Chennai, the modern name for Madras. Cassia bark (cinnamon), fenugreek, black pepper and turmeric are often added to the diversity, but no doubt Louisa would have bought the powder over the counter from a spice grocer.

Finger foods were not restricted to starters. They also served as fiddling foods during the inevitable after-dinner exchange of light conversational pleasantries. Take the following excerpt from the same chapter as an example

The suckling pig had vanished, the bones gleamed white in the joints of lamb and boar, and the rib cages and breast bones of the chickens and turkeys and ducks lay like the wreckage of upturned boats. Jeejee, having sampled a little of everything, at Mother's insistence, and having declared it infinitely superior to anything he had ever eaten before, was vying with Theodore to see how many Taj Mahal Titbits they could consume.

'Delicious,' muttered Jeejee indistinctly, his mouth full. 'Simply delicious, my dear Mrs Durrell. You are the apotheosis of culinary genius.'

'Yes, indeed,' said Theodore, popping another Taj Mahal Titbit into his mouth and scrunching it up. 'They're really excellent. They make something similar in Macedonia . . . er . . . um . . . but with goat's milk.'

Taj Mahal Titbits are really nothing more exotic than slices or fingers of spicy cheese on toast, commonly sold by road-side vendors to pilgrims and visitors to the Taj Mahal and other major heritage sites in northern India. Paneer, the acid-set Indian cheese made by curdling milk in either lemon juice or vinegar, is traditionally used, but as the recipe below indicates, Louisa was able to adapt the ingredients to use local sources given that the onion and chilli mask any taste the cheese might impart. One option might have been a hard, rather bland Greek cheese called *kasseri*. The goat's milk cheese that Theo referred to was probably *sirene*, a white brine cheese rather similar to feta, typical of the Balkans, often made with a combination of sheep's and cow's milk. It is interesting to note the specification for wheat bread, a feature which prob-ably derives from the fact that many different grains were used in India, and that the typical country subsistence bread of Corfu was made with maize flour.

## Taj Mahal Titbits

*Slices of toasted wheat bread*
*8 oz cheese, grated – paneer is best,*
*but Greek kasseri will do, feta also*
*2 spring onions chopped*
*1 green chilli finely chopped or grated*
*Pinch of cracked black pepper*
*1 tbsp olive oil*

Mix and mash the cheese, spring onions, chilli and black pepper in a bowl and make a stiff paste with the olive oil. Then spread thickly on toast and brown under a grill till bubbling. Cut into fingers and serve.

The third finger food is Tamarind Baida Roti, in reality nothing more than eggy bread rolls filled with tamarind chutney; it's a recipe that Louisa could easily have concocted. The eggs were readily available from the domestic fowl that were free-range in the villa garden; she had a recipe for chappatis from the 1887 manuscript and her recipe for tamarind chutnee [*sic*] is in the handwritten Dulwich College notebook. The chutney is made from the pureed, edible pulp of the pod-like fruits of the leguminous tree *Tamarindus indica*, a native of tropical Africa. Its sour and tart fruit is very popular in Indian cuisine.

## Tamarind Baida Roti

*4 leftover chapattis, cut into 3-inch rounds*
*4 eggs, beaten*
*salt and pepper to taste*
*1 cup of cooking oil*
*tamarind chutney filling*

Mix the eggs and chutney in the cooking oil; spread the mixture on the chapatti rounds and cook under a grill until the egg sets firm.

Finally, to complete the quartet, Louisa had often used a simple recipe called Tomatoes Indian from the early days of family life back in Jamshedpur when Gerry was a toddler. It was literally a double dose of the fruit, both fresh and as chutney. Traditionally, the recipe was as follows:

## Tomatoes Indian

Make a light batter with ½ pint milk, plain flour and one beaten egg. Take 1lb fresh tomatoes, cut into thin slices and dust with salt, pepper and curry powder. Dip the tomato slices in batter and bake on a tray in a medium oven for ten minutes. Fry rounds of old bread, spread with tomato chutney, put tomato fritters on them and sprinkle with parsley. Cut into finger–sized bites and serve hot.

# Indian Budgees:
## a Tasty Phonetic Transliteration

The Western World may now well know them universally as onion bhajis, but to the memsahibs of the Indian Raj, the spicy, crispy fritters based on onion, the most common bulb vegetable grown in the subcontinent, they were Indian budgees. The budgee was a favourite as a party starter, a comfort food in the rainy season and a popular children's snack in the nursery. There is a recipe for Indian budgees in Memsahib Durrell's cookbook and we might begin with an explanation of the variations in the spelling of the name, so that the tasty staple morsel may have a more attractively palatable and mouth–watering appeal.

The transliteration of Hindi into English was predominantly based upon phonetic interpretation of sounds and rhythms, particularly in respect of the vowels and the way in which they were pronounced in the native tongue. The visual representation of speech sounds (phones) nowadays uses a standard International Phonetic Alphabet which has evolved over the last three centuries. Different phonetic alphabets were applied in different parts of the colonial world in the eighteenth and nineteenth centuries and the Hindi-English translation/transliteration posed considerable problems. One specific example was the representation of the soft phonetic Hindi sound for the letter 'a' as the letter 'u' in written English. Here are some examples from the English dictionary that are in everyday use.

| bungalow | *bangalo* | a Bengali house |
|---|---|---|
| chutney | *chatni* | to crush |
| cummerbund | *kamarband* | a waist binding |
| jungle | *jangal* | a forest or wilderness |
| punch | *panch* | from the Hindi for 'five', the number of ingredients in the drink |
| pundit | *pandit* | a learned scholar or priest |
| thug | *thagi* | a thief, or a conman |

And so, these words lead us to budgee, transliterated through 'bagee,' 'badgee' and 'bhagee' to bhaji (regionally, 'bhajji,' 'bajji' and 'bhujia'), the familiar modern spelling, accepted in Indian cuisine throughout the Western world. Here is a transcription of Louisa's original recipe.

## Indian Budgees

*Lard, 1½ pounds for frying*
*6 ounces of self-raising flour*
*6 ounces of wholemeal or pea flour*
*2 ounces of margarine or dripping*

1 teaspoon of curry powder
1 teaspoon of salt
¼ teaspoon of chillies
1 egg, well beaten
2 onions, chopped (spring onions), part of the green to be used

Mix the dry ingredients with the dripping as cake. Add onions, egg and milk. Have the lard boiling. Drop spoons full of the mixture into the pan with the deep lard. A wire basket is best used for lifting out when a nice brown.

The recipe as written calls for some comments. First, milk is omitted from her list of ingredients and, in practice, it has been found that a tablespoon added to the beaten egg is more than sufficient. Then, the purists might have several criticisms of the combinations of both flours and fats. The use of self-raising flour removes the need to add baking soda – as some traditional recipes recommend; and the alternative of either wholemeal or pea (chickpea) flour – aka gram flour – may also raise an eyebrow, many recipes suggesting the use of both white and gram flour. The latter, aka *besan* flour, is usually produced from the type of small chickpea known as chana dhal and is often traditionally preferred for use on its own. Sometimes rice flour is added for a crispier product.

Lard for frying and beef dripping for the mixture may have been the original fatty substances used, but health concerns in the second half of the twentieth century have witnessed a change to either corn oil, or nowadays, rapeseed oil, which is virtually omnipresent in the off-the-shelf packets of the chilled supermarket product. Also, the use of a premixed curry powder may be frowned upon, rather than individual spices, like coriander, cumin, turmeric, and garlic or ginger. But, after all, one should realise that the recipe as published is an Anglo-Indian derivative of the true native snack or starter, which varied regionally anyway.

As far as the predominant ingredient, onions, are concerned, some authors specify the yellow variety, others white and a few recommend red. Very few, if any, suggest the use of spring onions, including the green shoots, as Memsahib Durrell does. In India, this bulb vegetable (*Allium cepa*), *piyaz* in Hindi, is a winter crop which is subject to the vagaries of climate and often fails to reach maturity as the familiar swollen bulb. Excess rainfall in November and its lack in January can affect the crop, but there are usually slender green shoots available. These are often referred to as 'spring onions' or scallions (*Allium cepa var. cepa*) and are essentially young plants that are harvested before the bulb begins to form. Another related species is the Welsh onion (*Allium fistulosum*), a common sight in both Indian and European gardens and one which also goes under the name of 'spring onion'. In Asia, generally, this species is of primary importance, both as a salad onion and in cooked dishes.

# Curry Puffs and Spicy Pasties

Gerry made reference to 'curry puffs' in the first chapter of *Fillets of Plaice*, entitled 'The Birthday Party'. This occasion was the eve of Louisa's fiftieth birthday and the Durrell family and friends had decided to take her on a short holiday cruise down the coast of the Greek mainland, the rather primitive region of Thesprotia, which had been under Ottoman rule until 1913 and was destined only to be granted official Greek regional status in 1937. The family had hired the motorboat, or *benzina*, of local fisherman Taki and the party sailed east-wards across the strait from Corfu harbour with Sven playing his accordion and Theodore vigorously singing 'There Is a Tavern in the Town'. The boat was beached, its anchor thrown safely into the strand of white sand, and the icebox was unpacked of its legs of lamb, lobsters and various extraordinary things Mother had made which she called curry puffs. Some of them were in fact curry puffs, but others were stuffed with different delicacies.

As the name suggests, the recipe requires the use of puff pastry, the making of which is a rather laborious and time-consuming process. Nevertheless, Louisa seems to have always made her own; here is her recipe.

## Puff Pastry

Take 6 oz of plain flour and mix with a pinch of salt on to a floured board. Make a well in the centre and gradually add a teaspoonful of lemon juice mixed with cold water to make a soft, moist dough. Knead with fingertips until smooth. Meanwhile work 6oz butter in a basin with a wooden spoon until soft. Roll the dough into an oblong and spread butter lightly over half the surface. Fold the unbuttered dough over the rest and press together to enclose the butter; moisten the edges with milk. Turn the pastry half round, roll again lightly into a strip and fold it into three. Press the sides to seal then turn again and repeat the process another five times, allowing five minutes between each folding and rolling. Wrap in greaseproof paper and keep in an icebox overnight.

## Curry Puffs

Take two sheets of ready-rolled puff pastry. Mix the following ingredients in a bowl:

*1 tbsp olive oil*
*2 spring onions, chopped*
*1 red chilli, chopped fine*

*2 garlic cloves, crushed*
*1 tsp grated fresh ginger*

Fry for 2–3 minutes, then turn back into the bowl and add 4oz minced chicken, 4oz mashed potato and 4 tbsp fresh chopped coriander, salt and pepper to taste. Use a 3-inch cutter to make rounds of puff pastry and place 1 tbsp of mixture on each round. Brush edges of round with a beaten egg, fold pastry over and crimp edges with a fork. Place parcels on a baking tray and cook in a hot oven for 15–20 minutes or until golden-brown and puffed.

The traditional recipe for the familiar Cornish pasty is one that combines a savoury minced beef and potato mixture at one end and a sweet apple and sultana mix at the other. Louisa went a few steps further in following her own recipe for a Spicy Pasty by omitting the minced beef and adding a dash of curry powder at the savoury end and pinches of cinnamon and nutmeg at the sweet end. The purists will probably not be too impressed, but it appears that the Durrell family enjoyed their mother's improvisation.

## Louisa's Spicy Pasty

Prepare rough puff pastry the day before, roll out thinly and cut into rounds about the diameter of a small pudding plate. Mix 4oz cold mashed potatoes and cooked carrot cubes and place on one quarter of each pastry round; add salt and pepper and a pinch of curry powder to taste. On the adjacent quarter, heap the cooked apple and sultana mix with a pinch of cinnamon and nutmeg combined. Fold the other half of the pastry round over the two mixtures, moisten the edges with milk and turn the lower edge over the upper. Prick randomly with a fork, brush with a little milk and bake in a quick oven until browned.

## *Mezes and Hortopitakia*

The well-known Greek version of small-plate food is the meze, often rendered in the plural as mezes, but actually *mezethes*. Literally translated the word means a taste or a bite and is used to describe small savoury snacks and finger foods that are served as complements to drinks. Ouzo and meze are usually considered to be the perfect partners, but traditionally, as in the days of Lawrence Durrell, Gostan Zarian, Theodore Stephanides and the intellectual literati of Corfu in the 1930s, the partnership was meze and retsina. At the so-called Ionian Banquets, instituted in the low-vaulted basement of the Perdika (Partridge) restaurant in Corfu Town, the toasts at the initiation dinner were first 'Retsina', followed by the exclamation 'Zito!', translated as either 'Hurrah!' or 'Long live!'.

In her collection, Louisa has a list of meze appetisers, but for only one was there an actual recipe, namely *skordalia*, a firm favourite of both Larry and Gerry for many years to come.

## Skordalia

Boil 500g potatoes in their skins; drain, peel and mash through a fine sieve. Crush two cloves of garlic to a paste with a pinch of salt and mix into the mashed potatoes. Mix juice of one small lemon with 140ml olive oil and beat slowly into the potatoes. Spread the *skordalia* thus made on to a dish and garnish with either crushed almonds or chopped walnuts. [Gerry preferred almonds and Larry walnuts.]

Then, there was batter-fried courgette (*kolokythakia tiganita*); Indian spiced sweet-potato cakes; cheese aubergine rolls (*bourekakia melitzanas*); spiced eggy bread with tomatoes (*kagianas*); and dolmades, always a favourite Greek meze, annotated with the word '*horta*' or 'vegetable' implying that her version used the familiar vine-leaf wrap to form a parcel of rice mixed with wild greens, omitting minced meat and making it suitable for her vegetarian daughter, Margo.

It was apparently for the dietary peculiarities of Margo that Louisa developed her knowledge of *hortopitakia*, small savoury turnovers made with fillings of aromatic herbs and greens (*horta*) and cheese. The most commonly encountered are known as spanakopita, (*spanakopitakia* or *spanakotyropita*) – spinach and cheese pie, or filo pastry triangles filled with a mixture of feta cheese and spinach. (*Tiropitakia* are miniature cheese pies, generally without herbs.) There are several references in *The Corfu Trilogy* to Louisa wandering away from a family picnic, rambling out from the villa into the surrounding olive groves, trug basket in hand, and returning with an assortment of wild greens with which to experiment in her kitchen. This practice continues today in the rural areas of Corfu and Greece in general and at least eighty different plant species can be identified as components of *horta*.

The nature of *horta* varies from region to region and season to season according to the availability of wild greens. In early spring in Corfu, it is dominated by asparagus and nettles, while a harvest in mid May is more diverse. Wild fennel and common sowthistle form the bulk of the foliage and there are smaller quantities of hartwort, hawksbeard and black nightshade, the latter a most surprising inclusion on account of its classification with other poisonous members of the nightshade family (*Solanaceae*). The most common *horta* dish in Corfu is *tsigareli*, in its true form comprising wild greens sauteed with garlic and hot pepper and served over polenta.

Louisa became aware that there were several obvious groups of wild relatives of familar garden vegetables with similar flavours which might be used as substitutes. For example, the most familiar culinary plant of this family of the family *Amaranthaceae* is spinach (*spanaki*, *Spinacia oleracea*) and many of its wild relatives have similar nutritional properties. *Vlita* is the amaranth or pigweed. Many species of amaranthus, such as *A. hybridus*, are native to North America and have been imported as garden crops or as weeds, but *A. blitum* and *A. graecizans* are both native to the eastern Mediterranean region. *Kokkinogoulia* or sea beet (*Beta vulgaris ssp. maritima*), is much sought after along the coast. Similarly, the garden weed *Chenopodium album*, known in English as lamb's quarters or fat hen, often features in *horta* dishes.

In the daisy family (*Asteraceae*), the Greek word *radikia*, is used for chicory (*Cichorium intybus ssp. intybus*), commonly cultivated in orchards, as well as yellow-flowered dandelion-like plants with a basal rosette of toothed leaves are collectively called *picralitha*. Dandelion (*Taraxacum*), is sometimes specifically called *galatsida*, but included under this general name are many other related plants, such as *zogos* or *zochos*, the common sowthistle (*Sonchus oleraceus*), which as the English name suggests is suitable only for pigs. This weakly prickled, fleshy-leaved, yellow-flowered plant, like the dandelion, exudes a bitter white liquid known as a latex that might seem singularly unattractive to the more refined palate. It is, however, a close relative of the common lettuce (*Lactuca sativa*), some varieties of which will also release milky latex when cut, hence the Latin name to imply lactation.

Wild relatives of carrot and parsley are still often much sought after. Leaves of wild carrot or *stafilinakas* (*Daucus carota*) and several other species from the carrot family (*Apiaceae*) are popular, especially the early growths of *marathos agrios*, the wild fennel (*Foeniculum vulgare*) and its close relative giant fennel (*Ferula communis*). Louisa regularly used fennel in her vegetarian pies.

Here is a recipe for a version of Louisa's *hortopitakia*. The species collected were those of which Louisa had a note – *radiki*, *galatsida* and *marathos* – chicory, dandelion and fennel. A note of caution is worthy of mention. Whereas Louisa could have foraged freely and without fear of contamination of her pickings, the vegetation beneath the olive trees is sometimes nowadays sprayed with a commercial herbicide to reduce weed growth and facilitate easier harvest of the olive fruit. The owners of such olive groves have the habit of indicating to the general public that the herbage has been sprayed by affixing an empty herbicide container to a wooden pole in a prominent position at the edge of the grove. So, always look for the white plastic container and pick elsewhere!

## Hortopitakia

Sauté one generous handful of fennel, one of mixed chicory and dandelion, and three finely chopped scallions in olive oil. Add ½ cup of water and simmer for 20 minutes. Then add one handful chopped spinach and cook for another five minutes. Drain well, then add one minced clove of garlic and 2 tsp ground cumin. Roll out puff pastry and cut into circles. Place a spoonful of *horta* mixture on one half of the pastry circle. Fold over the other half and pinch the edges with a fork. Heat ⅓ cup of olive oil and fry on both sides to a light golden colour. Set aside to drain on a rack with absorbent paper.

# 5

# A Culinary Heritage of the Durrell Family in Corfu

Mama Kondos and her Family. Mama (left), Giver of Snacks of Charcoal-roast Sweet Potato, Green Figs and Cornbread to Gerry; Maize Cobs and Watermelon Mush for Sally. (Gerry in Wellington Boots and Margo second right.)

Louisa Durrell was a 49-year-old widow when she brought her family to Corfu in 1935 from the suburbs of Bournemouth, England. Her eldest son and his wife had recently left home, attracted by the letters of friends, and she had made the bold decision to follow with her three younger children, aged 18, 16 and 10. She did not have a place to live and had to spend time in a pension in town before she could locate a villa with a reliable supply of water and a bathroom.

Amidst the political and economic uncertainty of the 1930s, she was required to manage a household for her family through its effective stay of five years on the island. From June 1935 to August 1939, she rented three quite different villas in the villages outside Corfu Town – Perama, Kontokali and Criseda – presumably, each better appointed in terms of space and facilities, and each appropriate to her financial situation. The basic requirements were a constant water supply, strong enough to service a bathroom, and a fully functional kitchen with comfortable and convenient cooking and storage facilities. To many people, the mere fact that she had to establish and operate three different kitchens in a period of five years is an absolutely daunting challenge, disruptive of a normal and relaxed family existence. But this is exactly what she under-took, clearly with excellent effect, if the tales from *The Corfu Trilogy* and the examination of the following recipes are to be taken as evidence.

All three villas lacked electricity and each of the kitchens had cooking ranges which relied on olive wood and charcoal as fuel. An essential aspect of this lifestyle was the provision of clean, potable water, a feature that was often taken for granted, especially in the context of Corfu in the 1930s when a general municipal mains water supply did not exist. This topic was one of the main concerns of Larry and he became something of a connoisseur on the subject. In a hot Mediterranean climate, a linking thread moves on from the water supply to the need for adequate refrigeration facilities, an icebox, to be replenished regularly with large blocks of ice brought from town by Spiro 'Americanos'. Being perhaps the most humid of all the Mediterranean islands, the kitchens of Corfu needed dry and secure storage facilities for such staple commodities as flour, bread and rice. And fourthly, it would be most advantageous if fresh foods, such as vegetables, eggs and honey, could be produced from the garden or orchard of the villas.

These four aspects are the basic, practical management facets of everyday existence that are important in the estab-lishment of a comparatively comfortable lifestyle. And, moreover, they contribute to an intriguing ecological home environment for an inquisitive young zoologist to both extend his studies and, in so doing, make some small practical contributions to the functioning of a household and its facilities.

## *Water: Taken for Granted*

When one reads Gerry's descriptions of his mother spending an inordinate length of time in the kitchen, either cooking from tried-and-tested recipes, or experimenting with new concoctions by reference to the latest cookbook she had acquired, one inevitably conjures up an image based upon one's own practical experiences in the kitchen. Inevitably, it is bound to be inaccurate and biased and, regrettably, there is a lack of a specific description of any one of the kitchens in the three Corfiot villas in *The Corfu Trilogy*. There are, however, snippets and titbits, throwaway comments and incidental asides, which permit their assembly into a framework of understanding of the essential practical characteristics of Louisa's favourite environment; and there are enthralling and mischievous tales to tell about the deeds and doings of Gerry and his siblings, and of visitors to the household.

First to be answered, there was the question about perhaps the most essential ingredient of cuisine – water. An interview of Margo (MD) by Susan and Ian MacNiven (IMN), *Margaret Durrell Remembers . . . A Dialogue in Corfu*, taken in 2000, reveals more about its availability.

IMN: What was the daily housekeeping like on Corfu?
We all run around here now with our bottles of water.
Did you have bottled water back in 1935?

MD: No, we didn't, but we had wonderful wells, and
buckets, and we never suffered from lack of water.

IMN: Did Larry drink water too?

MD: No, he added wine to his! It was a dreadful thing
to do!

Margo probably reacted thus because Larry had remarked that
an especially endearing quality of the locals was that they had
so delicate a palate as to be connoisseurs of cold water and
that the ubiquity of a glass of water at dinner tables suggested
an almost biblical significance. He noted that when a Greek
from the rural areas drank water he tasted and savoured it,
then told of which wells were the sweetest; similarly, the
townsfolk could identify the source of the water offered for
sale by each of the white itinerant handcarts. In like manner,
there was always a jug of water and glasses at Louisa's dinner
tables, for Larry to either savour or add it to his wine in the
true fashion of the Ancient Greeks.

Larry and Nancy were not as fortunate as the rest of the
family in that, at their home in the White House in Kalami,
all their water had to be carried down from a spring on the
high road a quarter of a mile up the ravine, in large earthen
jars on the backs of local womenfolk. The couple employed
a dowser to find water closer at hand, but he concluded
the supply was more than five metres below the surface and

thus too deep to abstract economically. Larry's friend Gostan Zarian, an Armenian novelist, suggested he employ a system for converting salt water into fresh, while Theodore Stephanides talked of the virtues of a method he had seen in operation in Macedonia where the locals constructed reservoirs by burying a pulp of the spongy stems and leaves of prickly pear cactus in a hole to the depth of two metres. The hole was then filled with clean pebbles and when the rains fell, the prickly pear soaked up the water and retained it in its spongy tissue. This system was best for walled garden–boxes and as a supply of water for general use in the kitchen, like cooking and washing up, but not as a source of drinking water.

In complete contrast, there was an enviable supply of sweet water when Larry and Nancy came to live at the Villa Anemoyanni for a couple of months, and one of the main discussion points was whether Gerry should keep his water snakes in the bath or in one of the larger kitchen cooking utensils. There is a good description of both the kitchen and the well in 'The Olive Merry-Go-Round' in *Birds, Beasts and Relatives*, in the tale of the occasion Larry's friends, Max and Donald, rowdy and drunk as ever could be, came to visit at two o'clock in the morning, inevitably waking the whole household. Max lit one of the charcoal fires in the kitchen with a five-pound note and a kettle was beginning to sing when the group suddenly noticed the absence of their friend. It turned out that Donald had fallen down the well and was clinging on to the central pipe. Larry's reaction was typically forthright and more concerned with the purity of the water supply than the possibility his drunken friend might drown.

'Donald, don't be a bloody fool,' said Larry exasperatedly. 'Come up out of there. If you fall into that water, you'll drown. Not that I worry about that, but you'll pollute our entire water supply.'

Donald and Max sent a huge box of chocolates and an apology to Mother the following morning.

## *Spiro and the Icebox; Gerry and the Ice Cream*

Iceboxes and freezers of American manufacture were common-place items of kitchen equipment in many middle-class households of the Indian Raj and, apparently, Louisa had the benefits of an icebox for most of her married life back in India. The White Mountain Company had been founded in New England in 1853 and had patented an ice cream maker by 1923, while Gem freezers had been manufactured by the American Machine Company of Philadelphia since 1889. However, refrigerators and freezers were uncommon sights in most Corfiot domestic kitchens and Louisa was most desirous to have what she considered to be such a vital piece of equipment.

Spiro 'Americanos' had been used to such gadgets during his time in Chicago and with a sketchy outline design from Louisa, he was soon at work on the project. 'Leaves its to me, Mrs Durrells,' he said, and such was his ingenuity that it did not take him long to fabricate a workable model. With the icebox fully functional and readily sustained by huge, coffin-shaped blocks of ice wrapped in sacking, brought regularly from town by Spiro, Louisa could turn her energies to experimenting with the making and preservation of ice cream. Her basic recipe using an egg, half a pint of milk, sugar and vanilla essence, was as follows:

## Ice Cream

Beat the egg and stir together with the warmed milk, add sugar to taste and pour the mixture into a slender jug. Stand the jug in a saucepan of boiling water over the fire and stir until the mixture thickens into a custard, taking care that it does not boil, or it will turn lumpy. Cover and stand it in a cool spot in the kitchen. Add a few drops of vanilla essence and once it has become quite cold, decant into smaller bowls or moulds, and pack them around with ice in the icebox.

Louisa had added two notes to the end of this recipe. The first read: 'Almond essence, grated chocolate, grated rind of a lemon, or a tablespoonful of strawberry preserve and cochineal, may be used to make an assortment of flavours.' The second seemed to be an adult recipe which stated that as a second stage to the custard concoction, Italian ice cream required mixing in a teaspoonful of finely grated lemon rind, the juice of two lemons, a pint of cream, a wine-glass of brandy, a wine-glass of *crème de noyaux* (an almond-flavoured liqueur made from apricot kernels), and half a pound of sugar, before freezing. In spite of his mother's dexterity in producing a diversity of types of ice cream, Gerry usually had to request her to make a batch on demand, and rarely were they readily available in the icebox when he came in from his expeditions. He did, however, have an alternative source.

In *The Garden of the Gods*, Chapter 6, 'The Royal Occasion', he tells of his visits to the tiny café of his friend, Costi Avgadrama, who was famous for producing the best ice cream in Corfu and who had been commissioned to concoct a special ice cream for the visit of King George II of Greece to the island in May 1936. Gerry was in the habit of visiting the café regularly, to fulfil a working agreement with Costi: 'I would go to his café three times a week to collect all the cockroaches in his kitchen to feed to my birds and animals, and in return for this service I was allowed to eat as many ice creams as I could during my work.' In the first main chapter of *The Amateur Naturalist*, 'The Naturalist on Home Ground', Gerry describes the resident fauna of one of the Corfiot villas in which the family lived in the late 1930s.

In the big stone kitchens, where my mother cooked on charcoal fires and it was warm and dry, there was a little creature resembling the silverfish called by the charming name of the firebrat. In this area of the house, we also had two species of cockroach, against which my mother waged a constant unsuccessful battle. I was fascinated by their beauty, for to me they looked as though they were carved out of tortoiseshell and their egg cases were so elegant, like the most beautiful little ladies' evening hand-bags. I used to collect these capsules and hatch them out in my room (unbeknownst to my mother); half I would let go and the other half I would feed to my mantis, gecko, tree frogs and so on – I felt this was fair.

Gerry demonstrates an intimate knowledge of these insect pests as evidenced by line drawings of a cockroach with an egg case; cockroach droppings for comparison with those of housefly, house mouse and rat; and an account and diagram of a dissection headed 'Inside the Cockroach'. The two species to which he refers were almost certainly the larger two of the four commonly encountered in European kitchens: at a size range of 20–30mm in length, the American cockroach (*Periplaneta americana*) and the oriental cockroach (*Blatta orientalis*). *Katsarida* is the general Greek word for all species of cockroach. For the record, the firebrat (*Thermobia domestica*) and the silverfish (*Lepisma saccharina*), mentioned in Gerry's excerpt above, belong to a group of wingless insects, commonly called bristletails.

As to the constant battle Mrs Durrell was waging against these harmless household pests, the very chemicals of destruction were readily available in her kitchen and she had a recipe for just that task. A saucer containing a mixture of sugar and baking soda could be set in a warm, dark corner, next to another saucer filled with water. The insects were attracted by the sweetness of the sugar, ate the mixture and then took a drink. The hydration of the mixture caused fermentation, the release of carbon dioxide, which built up internal pressure in the insect's body and eventually caused it to explode! Natural history, entomology, ecology begins at home and the special bond between mother and son was laid down in this familiar environment and strengthened for life.

## *Care with the Storage and Cooking of Rice*

For many of the savoury dishes Louisa cooked in India and in England, certainly all her curries, she used the long-grain *indica* variety of rice, widely known as basmati, the Hindi word for 'fragrant'. It was grown throughout the subcontinent, and in the region of the Upper Ganges around her birthplace of Roorkee, it was known as *dehradun*. It had been readily available to buy in English shops but it was comparatively hard to come by in Greece, especially Corfu, though the former British influence in the Ionian Islands had created an awareness of the variety. One of the reasons for this uncommonness was the fact that only the short-grained *japonica* varieties were grown in northern mainland Greece and Italy. The Greek and Venetian cuisine used mainly short-gained *arborio* rice imported from the Po valley, of northern Italy, or *vialone nano*, a variety native to Veneto and the paddy fields of Bassa Veronese, the plains that extend south from Verona. Generally known as risotto rice, the Venetian heritage of Corfu determined its use as an accompaniment for roast game birds, the stuffing for dolmades (vine-leaf parcels) and sweet rice puddings. The niceties of the different varieties of short-grained *japonica* rice passed Louisa by, for she merely had a recipe for 'Italian rice'. Spiro was apparently able to find a reasonably constant supply of long-grain rice in Corfu Town, but its relative rarity seems to have led Louisa to pay special attention to its storage and cooking. Here are some of her notes.

Storage: When storing rice, preferably use a glass container with a tightly sealed lid, kept in a cool, dry, dark location in the kitchen, such as in a wall cabinet, rather than a floor cupboard.

The storage jars should be examined regularly for the presence of insect pests by rotating and shaking the grain. If infestation is suspected, place storage jars in the icebox for a week and re-examine. Remove dead bodies.

This would have been a task Gerry took it upon himself to do intermittently, searching for the larvae and adults of such insects as the rice weevil (*Sitophilus oryzae*), a small red-brown beetle a mere 2–4mm in size, and the Indian meal moth (*Plodia interpunctella*).

Whole grain does not keep as long as refined or pearled grain because the germ portion with its natural oil content causes the grain to gradually become rancid. Uncooked brown rice should not be kept more than six months. Uncooked white can be kept indefinitely.

Flavoured rice may be made by placing a dry spice such as a cinnamon stick, cardamom or a nutmeg in the storage jar.

Cooked rice, white or brown, may be stored in the icebox, but should be used in three to four days.

The storage cupboards for grain and flour may be strewn with the twigs and leaves of the bay laurel (*Laurus nobilis*) to act as a mild insecticide. The supply of eggs from the family's domestic fowl was evidently sufficient for Louisa to make her own floor polish. Here is her recipe.

## Polish for Floors and other Wooden Surfaces

Beat up an egg (white & yellow together); slowly stir in quarter of a pint of vinegar, then stir in a quarter pint of turpentine. Shake well for half an hour and add a little powdered camphor (say 3 grams) to prevent mouldiness. This latter ingredient should be omitted for kitchen tables but a little may be used for shelves on which storage jars stand.

Whether it was because the supplies of long-grain rice were not easily sourced or whether because it was comparatively dear when compared to prices in India, Louisa took great care in the cooking and presentation of this vital companion of many dishes, often treated with some disdain. She obviously viewed it as a commodity that was just as important as the chicken in chicken curry. Here are her meticulous rules for preparing perfect rice.

## Stepwise Boiling Rice for Curries

Take a two-quarts (four-pints) pan, three parts filled with water, with the juice of half a lemon and a dessertspoonful of salt, then set to boil. Take two to three ounces of uncooked rice and sieve, but do not wash. Place a small jug of cold water within easy reach of the cooking stove. When the water is boiling freely, add the rice and stir gently with a wooden spoon. Note the time when the rice was put in the boiling water and after ten or twelve minutes begin to test the grains by taking a few out and pinching them between finger and thumb. When the grains feel thoroughly softened but firm, stop the boiling at once by throwing in the jug of cold water and remove the pan from the heat. Strain and drain the rice through a metal sieve. Return the rice to the pan, shake well and set it on a hot plate. Cover with a clean napkin and repeat shaking now and then to separate the grains and free those grains still attached to the sides of the pan. Scatter the grains with a fork; never use a spoon. The drying process will take from eight to ten minutes and must not be hurried; a good cook always allows time for this operation. Well-boiled rice will not be brought to the table in a satisfactory state unless it has been drained and dried as above.

A scribbled note on Louisa's instructions reads 'Kenney-Herbert', suggesting that she would have been following the instructions of Colonel Arthur Kenney-Herbert (1840–1916), a soldier in the British Indian Army (1859–1894). Kenney-Herbert wrote diverse books and articles on Anglo-Indian cuisine, beginning in 1879 with *Culinary Jottings from Madras: A Treatise on Reformed Cookery for Anglo-Indian Exiles*. Because of the military background of the Durrell family, there seems little doubt that his books would have been well read in that family. On retirement from the army, Kenney-Herbert founded the Common-Sense Cookery Association in 1894.

## *Chickens in the Garden, Honey in the Hive*

At the Strawberry-Pink Villa, Gerry would awake to the sun streaming through the barred shutters of his bedroom, accompanied by the sound of the melancholy bells, signifying that the goats were on their way to new pastures; of rousing cock-crows, and of the beckoning scent of charcoal from the kitchen ovens. Breakfast would be on its way and the morning's adventures could barely wait to be engaged. He describes the typical scene in Chapter 3 of *My Family and Other Animals*.

> We ate breakfast out in the garden, under the small tangerine trees. The sky was fresh and shining, not yet the fierce blue of noon, but a clear milky opal. The flowers were half asleep, roses dew-crumpled, marigolds still tightly shut. Breakfast was, on the whole, a leisurely and silent meal, for no member of the family was very talkative at that hour. By the end of the meal the influence of the coffee, toast, and eggs made itself felt, and we started to revive, to tell each other what we intended to do, why we intended to do it, and then argue earnestly as to whether each had made a wise decision.

Breakfasts were much the same at Villa Anemoyanni where the garden was large enough for Louisa to keep a small flock of domestic fowl and the family was generally self-sufficient in eggs which, at breakfast, were either consumed hard-boiled or scrambled. Occasionally, the tending of the hens was not so conscientious as it might have been, especially when it was Margo's turn to be their minder. There is an amusing description of breakfast in the Durrell household in the eponymous tale in *Marrying Off Mother and Other Stories* (1991), at a table set, as ever, in the shade of tangerine trees, by the Durrell's long-suffering maid, Lugaretzia. Gerry wrote:

> This day I had noted with satisfaction that we were having scrambled eggs. Mother used to simmer chopped onions until they were transparent and then add the beaten eggs that had yolks as brilliant as the sun and came from our own family of chickens. One day my sister Margo, in a philanthropic mood, let all the chickens out of their pen for a walk. They found a patch of wild garlic and feasted on it, with the result that the omelettes for breakfast the next morning were thoroughly impregnated. My brother Leslie complained that it was like eating the upholstery out of a Greek bus.

The species of wild garlic was no doubt the ubiquitous Neapolitan garlic (*Allium neapolitanum*), a far more pungent member of the onion family, generally best avoided as an alternative to the cultivated onion. It is interesting to note Louisa's habit of always incorporating sauteed chopped onions into both scrambled eggs and simple omelettes. As for the weird simile provided by Leslie, one wonders on how many occasions he had chewed the upholstery of a bus, nay, how many times he had actually been on a Greek bus?

Then there was the toast and honey. Gerry often followed his scrambled eggs with four or five huge slices of brown toast covered with a thick coating of honey from the family hives. For Gerry, breakfast was often much more than a mere meal.

Lest I be thought greedy, let me hasten to say that eating this much toast and honey was much like following a natural history lesson or an archaeological dig. The hives were in charge of Lugaretzia's husband, a fragile-looking man who seemed to have the cares of the world on his shoulders, as, indeed, he had, as anyone spending ten minutes in his wife's company would readily perceive. Whenever he deprived our five hives of bees of their carefully garnered provender he was always stung so severely that he would have to spend several days in bed. As he was being stung, however, he inevitably dropped several honeycombs on the ground, where they became a magnificent sticky trap for any insect that happened to be around. In spite of Mother's desperate attempts to strain the honey before it came to the table, there was always a small and interesting zoological collection lurking there. So, spreading the musky, brown-gold delicacy on your bread was like spreading out liquid amber in which you might find almost anything from tiny moths and caterpillars to beetles and small centipedes. Once, to my delight, I found a species of earwig that was unknown to me. So, breakfast was always a biologically interesting meal. The rest of my family, who, to my chagrin, remained defiantly unzoological, did not share my pleasure at the rich bounty the honey provided.

Gerry's Donkey, *Sally*, with Margo. Preparing to Visit
Countess Mavrodaki for a Sumptuous Five-course Lunch,
of Soup, Whitebait, Snipe, Wild Boar, and Meringue
with Champagne and Brandy.

# 6

# The Influence of
# Theodore Stephanides

Botany and Burfi beneath an Ancient Olive Tree.
Gerry and Alexia Stephanides Studying Plants and Eating
Indian Chocolate Fudge (burfi).

Theodore Stephanides (1896–1983) was a Greek polymath – poet, author, doctor (radiographer) and naturalist who was a great friend of the Durrell family and mentor of both Gerry and Larry. In his Corfu memoirs called *Autumn Gleanings*, he describes the chain of events that led him to meet the members of the Durrell Family. He had struck up a friendship with Larry's friend and Gerry's tutor, George Wilkinson, in the autumn of 1934 while hunting for field mushrooms in the olive woods around Analypsis and Kanoni. George spoke of the impending arrival of the Durrell family and in the summer of 1935, he and his wife Pamela invited Theodore to meet the Durrells for tea at the Strawberry-Pink Villa.

## *Discussions with Louisa*

It was not long before Theo became important to everyone. Gerry observed in *The Garden of the Gods*:

With Mother he could discuss plants, particularly herbs and recipes, while keeping her supplied with reading matter from his capacious library of detective novels.

Being born and having spent his adolescent years in Bombay, he had quite a grasp of the herbs that were used in the cuisine of western India and in the eastern Mediterranean, and their differences. One confusion which exercised Louisa's mind was the fact that the Indian bay was not the same plant as the European bay. In a couple of her recipes she had pencilled three words against the use of bay – 'Not Indian *tejpata*.' *Tej patta* is Hindi for the subtropical Indian bayleaf (*Cinnamomum tamala*) and not the familiar bay laurel (*Laurus nobilis*) of Mediterranean regions, commonly used in western European cuisine. Although both are members of the same family, *Lauraceae*, they are quite distinct in leaf type and aroma. A recipe Louisa had used in India flavoured with *tej patta* was *boondi ladoo*, a Rajasthani snack food made from sweetened chickpea flour rolled into small balls, a treat Theo knew of in childhood. Her attempts to recreate the recipe in Corfu were apparently unsatisfactory.

Theo could comment upon the similarities between Indian and Greek appetisers, such as Taj Mahal Titbits, which he was able to say had a related creation in Macedonia. He could identify the traditional dishes from the typical Corfiot cuisine of the times of the Venetian Empire, the various ways in which the Venetians cooked their favourite fish, the flathead grey mullet (*Mugil cephalus*), and in so doing, alert Gerry when there was going to be a fish-drive in Lake Chalikiopoulos. He could advise on such topics as the preparation of the scorpionfish and the careful removal of its poisonous spines before cooking.

As for Louisa's love of detective novels, Theo had a library in which those of the English crime author Anthony Berkeley Cox, writing under a variety of pen names, featured prominently. There are several in Louisa's archives. As Anthony Berkeley he caused his sleuth, Roger Sheringham, to investigate *The Silk Stockings Murders* (1928), *The Poisoned Chocolates Case* (1929) and *Panic Party* (1934). Meanwhile, in the guise of Francis Isles he had published *Malice Aforethought* (1931) and *Before the Fact* (1932), the latter a dastardly tale with murders on a country estate in Dorset near Bournemouth, using an unsuspected household cleaning fluid, and by the rapid consumption of a beaker of brandy in a brothel in Paris. Perhaps the novel which had the greatest effect on Gerry's writings was *Cicely Disappears* (1927), written by Berkeley under the pen name of A. Monmouth Platts, about the disappearance of a young woman from within a blacked-out room during an experimental seance, a topic guaranteed to engage Louisa's otherworldly interests. From where else would Gerry take the name Cicely for his pet praying mantis?

Often when Theo brought a different book for Louisa he would be accompanied by his daughter Alexia, who was either two or three years younger than Gerry. Like as not she and Gerry would roam through the garden of the villa while Louisa quickly mixed a quantity of Indian chocolate fudge known as *burfi* as a treat for the children and for Theo to take home to his wife Mary. She would, of course, also reserve some *burfi* fudge to accompany her adventure into her latest crime novel. The recipe uses tinned condensed milk, a ubiquitous feature of the kitchens of the Indian Raj from the mid-nineteenth century onwards and equally popular in England in the first half of the twentieth century. For Louisa it replaced the often difficult-to-acquire supplies of fresh milk and also satisfied the Durellian sweet tooth.

## Burfi Fudge

*3 cups sugar*
*3 tbsp cocoa powder*
*¼ tsp salt*
*12oz tin condensed milk*
*½ cup butter*
*1 tsp vanilla essence*

Combine sugar, cocoa and salt in a saucepan. Pour in condensed milk and mix well. Set the pan over medium heat and stir with a wooden spoon till the mixture boils. Remove from heat and wipe round to prevent sugar crystals forming above the mixture. Add butter and vanilla and beat with spoon for five minutes to incorporate. Pour into a greased pan and allow to cool and firm. Cut into bite-sized pieces.

## *Historical and Metaphysical Discussions with Larry*

Theodore had collected a wealth of historical knowledge on the simpler practical aspects of the sustenance of the island population through the various periods of colonial occupation. He could talk, for example, on the British influence in the Ionian Islands and of their contribution to the staple diet. He was familiar with the writings, from 1842, of John Davy, a British Inspector-General of Army Hospitals, who considered the value of the potato to be far too low for it to be profitably cultivated; he had noted it was not then used by the natives and he had expressed the hope that it never would be a principal article of food. He opined that a limited cultivation might only be a profitable crop in the vicinity of the principal military stations for the supply to the English inhabitants. As a footnote he stated that he had been informed of an attempt to introduce cultivation of the potato into Corfu by the Lord High Commissioner, Sir Howard Douglas, who ruled between 1835 and 1840. He had supplied the small farmers with seed potatoes provided they brought a certificate from the mayor of their village to witness that they had prepared a specified area of ground for their planting. Allegedly the offer was widely accepted, though in some instances abused, but nevertheless, it had only a limited effect in encouraging the cultivation of the crop.

The popularity of potatoes had grown considerably by the 1930s and often two crops were harvested annually. The first was planted in February at the start of spring and was ready by the end of May; the second planting was at various times from July to September and a local supply was ensured through winter. Theo had advised the Durrell family that there were two main dishes in which potatoes were used: *patates fourno* – literally oven-baked potatoes – baked in their skins with thyme and oregano; and *skordalia*, as described previously in Chapter 4. This dish was common as a meze and often eaten with fried salt cod on corn festivals such as 25 March (Lady Day), Palm Sunday, and on the Feast of the Transfiguration on 6 August.

Another religious festival with a food association was the Feast of St John the Baptist on Midsummer Eve (23 June), which was also celebrated as a Harvest Festival for the gathering in of maize or Indian corn, and the baking of new maize bread, or *bobota*. The corn had been sown at the end of October or early November and harvested at the end of May/June; on normal draining soils, it was cultivated in a larger proportion than wheat. A second crop would also grow on ground that had been waterlogged in winter, on deep, damp soils such as on the plains in the Ropa Valley. Sown in late spring (April), it flowered in June and was harvested towards the end of the hot season, chiefly in September. In the 1930s, maize constituted the principal article of the food of the labouring class on the island. Freshly ground dried corn with a granular texture, not ground as fine as cornflour or cornstarch, of a similar consistency to the Italian polenta, was used to make *bobota* for the staple meal of cornbread with feta cheese – *bobota me tyri*.

## Bobota Me Tyri

*2 cups (6oz) cornmeal*
*¼ cup (¾ oz) sugar*
*1 tsp baking powder*
*¼ cup (2 fl oz) olive oil*
*1 cup (2 tbsp) tepid water*

Mix cornmeal, sugar and baking powder in a dry bowl. In a separate bowl whisk oil and water until blended. Add liquid ingredients to dry ingredients and stir into a firm batter. Pour batter into an oiled pie pan and bake for 40–45 minutes, according to needle/toothpick test. Cool for 10 minutes before cutting into slices.

Larry was fascinated by Theo's knowledge of the cultivation of seasonal staples and their traditional use at religious festivals. Along with his friends from the Perdika (Partridge) restaurant, he also had a deeper thirst to acquire knowledge of presumed pagan rites such as the use of the offering of *colyva* in memory of a departed friend or relative. This is best exemplified by a passage from 'Landscape with Olive Trees' in *Prospero's Cell*, headed '15.1.38'.

During the last summer visit to the Count D, we attended a ceremony which furnished the seed for a whole train of arguments about pagan survivals, which since have been incorporated in one of Theodore's many unpublished monographs. The Count was half-way down the avenue of cypress trees when we came upon him, carrying in his hand a beautiful Venetian dish, full of something which only Theodore recognised as Colyva – the offering to the dead.

He said he was making a small reverence to a cousin who had died two years ago, on the anniversary of his death. He was continuing a prevalent peasant custom, descended from an ancient pagan rite. The contents of the dish of colyva were pomegranate seeds, wheat, pine nuts, almonds and raisins, all soaked in honey. 'Here, it really tastes rather nice. Try some.' They entered the chapel with the offering.

'There really is no need for the unearthly hush,' said the Count quietly. 'For us death is very much a part of everything. I am going to put this down here on Alecco's tomb to sustain his soul. Afterwards I shall offer you some more of it at home, my dear Zarian, to sustain your body. Is that not very Greek? We never move far in our metaphysical distinctions from the body itself. There is no incongruity in the idea that what fortifies our physical bowels, will also comfort Alecco's ghostly ones.

In contrast with his metaphysical inspiration for Larry, Theo was also on hand to advise Margo on her dietary programmes and unguent preparations for her acne. He could inform Leslie on shooting traditions on the island and talk expertly on the migratory movement of game birds such as the woodcock, turtle dove and members of the thrush family. He knew the best places and seasons for wild duck and brown hare, and he would inevitably punctuate all this advice with some of his characteristically whimsical puns, like, 'Is that your hare, or is it a wig?'

## Sowbread and Salepi: Polymath and Homeopath

Whenever the name of Theo Stephanides is mentioned, the word 'polymath' is usually applied in the same, or subsequent sentence. Originally from the Greek *polymathes*, then Latin *homo universalis*, a modern accepted definition might be 'a person whose expertise spans a significant number of subject areas or disciplines.' In the so-called impressionist travelogue, *The Colossus of Maroussi*, often considered to be the finest work of the American author, Henry Miller, Stephanides is described thus:

One day Theodore turned up – Dr. Theodore
Stephanides. He knew all about plants, flowers, trees,
rocks, minerals, low forms of animal life, microbes,

diseases, stars, planets, comets and so on. Theodore is the most learned man I have ever met, and a saint to boot.

Miller had been staying with Larry at the White House in Kalami in the September of 1939 and Theo's tales of serving in the First World War trenches of the Balkans with the poet George Katsimbalis inspired Miller to write about Katsimbalis as the eponymous 'colossus'. The other aspect of their encounters which Theo recalls in his *Autumn Gleanings* was Miller's interest in botany. He recalled in his memoirs that:

> Henry Miller, like Lawrence, took a great delight in the Corfu wildflowers, especially the lovely pink cyclamen which had just begun to appear before he left the island. During my stay at Kalami, he was constantly bringing me flowers of every shape and colour and asking me their names. Apparently, it came as a great surprise to him when he discovered that there were a good many specimens I could not name.

Miller recognised there were many different levels of knowledge in each subject for a person to be labelled a polymath. In the case of the cyclamen, for example, there was its etymology and variety of names: *kuklaminos* (Greek – from kuklos, a circle describing the shape of its tuberous root or corm; *cyclaminos* (Latin); *Cyclamen hederifolium* (its official Latin binomial); translated into English as ivy-leaved cyclamen; and into common or vulgar country language as sowbread. As this name suggests, its tubers were much sought after as a staple starchy foodstuff for both sexes of wild and domesticated pigs – sow and boar. The striking autumnal presence of the flowers is no better illustrated than in the title and contents of Chapter 15 in *My Family and Other Animals*.

Theo knew of the use of the tuberous corm of cyclamen as a human subsistence food during the First World War and the use of its leaves as an alternative to those of the vine for dolmades. His knowledge of medicinal plants would have extended to an understanding of the inclusion of small amounts of dehydrated and grated tubers in preparations to lessen anxiety, the debilitating impacts of migraine and blurred vision and in the regulation of the menstrual cycle.

Miller shared the proclivity of Larry and Nancy for naturism, regularly sunbathing nude in what they considered to be the normal style of the ancient Greeks. Theo did not emulate their tendency to public natural exposure but condoned the practice, pointing out that the word 'gymnasium' had a Greek origin and meant to 'train naked'. Miller also admired Theo's translation of many Greek love poems and songs into English, notably, the classic seventeenth-century romance *Erotokritos*, the work of the Cretan poet Vinkentios Kornaros. It was well known that both Henry and Larry were intrigued by erotica and Larry had arranged visits by Countess X with her troupe of nubile linguists, jugglers, acrobats and water nymphs undoubtedly with the aim of creating tableaux from an ancient Greek frieze. Henry wrote that 'things went whacky right from the start', identifying, in particular, Niki with the Nile green eyes and hair that seemed to be entwined with serpents.

Theo had already left, but no doubt had given Larry a supply of *salepi* powder, to make the drink that he was to go on to recommend to travellers in *Prospero's Cell*, thus: 'Salepi. Tea made from bulbs. Excellent. Swamp *orchis* provides the bulbs.' Popular throughout the Ottoman Empire, Theo had first come across it in Thessaloniki during the war when it was a popular sex potion and aphrodisiac of the soldiers, being dispensed by itinerant vendors on street corners. In later years he was to write a medicinal explanation. The bulbs to which Larry referred were actually the root tubers of various species of orchid, most commonly in Corfu, *Orchis italica*, variously known as Italian Orchid or Naked Man Orchid; and *Orchis* (*Anacamptis*) *laxiflora* – loose-flowered orchid. *Orchis* is the Greek word for 'testicle' which the paired, swollen tuberous roots resemble and by assumption of sympathetic similarity, an extract conferred male sexual potency. The tubers were dried, chopped and then ground to a fine flour. As with many traditional beliefs, modern pharmaceutical analysis has identified the active ingredients as water-soluble polysaccharides known as glucomannans. Here is a recipe as recommended by Theo and Dr Androuchelli.

## Salepi Tea

Stir 1 tbsp salepi flour into 1 cup of milk, sweetened with ½ tsp sugar, and simmer in a *briki* for 5–6 minutes until the mixture thickens. Pour into a cup and sprinkle with powdered cinnamon and/or ginger to taste.

# *Microscopy and Mischief with Gerry*

Examples of Theo's constant influence and inspiration for Gerry are littered throughout the books of *The Corfu Trilogy*, but probably a most insightful view of the polymath comes from an anecdote from Nancy via her daughter, about his relationship with Gerry and indirectly, his mischievous leg-pulling of Louisa and her culinary and supernatural fascinations (vide *Amateurs in Eden* by Joanna Hodgkin, Chapter 6 'Prospero's Island.')

Theodore's passion for wildlife was a godsend for Gerry, though among the locals he had earned a reputation as something of a witch doctor who concocted potions from pondlife, an accusation rooted in fact. He got the idea that microscopic organisms were a rich source of protein. To demonstrate this he occasionally dredged a whole lot up, drained them and made them into sandwiches. Nice, he declared, munching appreciatively, but no one else was tempted.

This would have been the popular view of Theo's Pond Life Sandwich, surely a gentle jibe in Louisa's direction, with her son, Gerry, as an accomplice. It might best be referred to as Theo's Shrimp and Cyclops Sandwich, for one has to remember that he was a scientist and a microscopist who had been employed by the Rockefeller Foundation to survey the water bodies of the island and identify the most important breeding grounds for the larvae of malaria-carrying mosquitoes, in advance of a spraying programme for the eradication of the disease. As a by-product of this research, he had published scientific papers on the freshwater flora and fauna of Corfu. He knew what organisms would be in a water sample from a particular lake and by simple sieving with a fine-mesh muslin, followed by immersion in gently boiling water, he could concoct the filling for the sandwich, having first checked the fauna microscopically. He would have demonstrated to Gerry the presence of minuscule and microscopic crustaceans, like water fleas (*Daphnia*), amphipods (*Gammarus*) and copepods (*Cyclops*), a nutritious freshwater zooplankton which comprised the smaller relatives of the familiar shrimps and prawns that graced many a dining table. This aspect is succinctly illustrated in Chapter 6 'The Sweet Spring' in *My Family and Other Animals*:

So, absorbed and happy, we would pore over the micro-scope. Filled with enthusiasm, we would tack from subject to subject, and if Theodore could not answer my ceaseless flow of questions himself, he had books that could. Gaps would appear in the bookcase as volume after volume was extracted to be consulted, and by our side would be an ever-growing pile of volumes.

'Now this one is a cyclops . . . *cyclops viridis* . . . which I caught out near Govino the other day. It is a female with egg-sacs . . . Now, I'll just adjust . . . you'll be able to see the eggs quite clearly . . . I'll just put her in the live box . . . er . . . hum . . . there are several species of cyclops found here in Corfu . . . '

Into the brilliant circle of white light a weird creature would appear, a pear-shaped body, long antennae that twitched indignantly, a tail like sprigs of heather, and on each side of it (slung like sacks of onions on a donkey) the two large sacs bulging with pink beads.

' . . . called cyclops because, as you can see, it has a single eye situated in the centre of its forehead. That's to say, in the centre of what *would* be its forehead if a cyclops had one. In Ancient Greek mythology, as you know, a cyclops was one of a group of giants . . . er . . . each of whom had one eye. Their task was to forge iron for Hephaestus.'

In many ways, Theo's Shrimp and Cyclops Sandwich was the ultimate spoof to tease the woman whose family he respected and loved for many years to come.

Nancy and Theo Discussing the Pond Life Sandwich

# 7

# The Delights of
# Afternoon Tea

Gerry's Magpies also Possessed the Durrellian Sweet Tooth

*. . . another of Mother's gastronomic triumphs.*

There is a most eloquent description of the fare Louisa served up for afternoon tea in *My Family and Other Animals*, Chapter 18, 'An Entertainment with Animals', which enables the composition of a perfect menu of recipes for a typical Durrellian afternoon tea. Gerry first puts the tea into context and then itemises the gastronomic attractions which were, no doubt, his own personal preferences. Let us recreate the afternoon menu while attempting to put each into a literary context in *The Corfu Trilogy*.

> Lunch over, the guests were too bloated with food to do anything except siesta on the veranda, and Kralefsky's attempts to organize a cricket match were greeted with complete lack of enthusiasm. A few of the more energetic of us got Spiro to drive us down for a swim, and we lolled in the sea until it was time to return for tea, another of Mother's gastronomic triumphs. Tottering mounds of hot scones; crisp, paper-thin biscuits; cakes like snowdrifts, oozing jam; cakes dark, rich and moist,

crammed with fruit; brandy snaps brittle as coral and overflowing with honey.

# *An Eloquence of Cakes*

Gerry's 'cakes dark, rich and moist, crammed with fruit' are undoubtedly the Indian Plum Cakes for which Louisa was so famous; while the 'cakes like snowdrifts, oozing jam' are less easy to identify. Of all the seventeen cakes in Louisa's cookbooks, the most likely candidate is probably her Light Layer Cake. Here are her appropriate recipes.

## Plum Cake (Indian)

The original manuscript copy of the recipe for this creation is on display in a cabinet in the Gerald Durrell Story in the Jersey Zoo. It is in a small dog-eared note-book and the page is foxed, smudged and bespattered to suggest that it was frequently consulted. It is three recipes in one with three quantities for each ingredient, halving by two steps, thus: flour 1lb or 8oz or 4oz. Transcribed is the recipe for the largest quantities to give some indication of the major undertaking.

*Flour 1lb*
*Butter 2lb*

*Sugar 1lb*

*Raisins 1lb*

*Sultanas 2lb*

*Ginger peel 1lb*

*Almonds 1lb*

*Paisley Flour 1 tablespoon*

*Mixed Spices 2 tablespoons*

*Brandy 1 wine glass*

*Eggs 1½ doz*

*Salt 2 teaspoons*

Butter well beaten to a cream with sugar. Add yolks of eggs one by one, then all the other ingredients, last of all whites beaten well (see manuscript copy of recipe on chapter 7 title page for details).

It should be possible to work from this original manuscript, but as a word of caution, the 4oz measures are adequate for a cake for one afternoon tea for four persons. There may be a need to reduce the quantities of the last five ingredients according to taste, but perhaps not the brandy! Incidentally, Paisley flour is another name for self-raising flour, the town in which it was first made by the Brown & Polson company. If a beach picnic is planned, make sure the cake is a part of the spread, as it was when the family picnicked on the beach below Pantocrator after picking grapes and drinking new wine, in the story told by Gerry in 'The Angry Barrels' chapter in *Birds, Beasts and Relatives*.

Under the influence of tea, buttered toast, salt biscuits, watercress sandwiches, and an enormous fruit cake as damp and as fragile and as rich-smelling as loam, we started to wake up. Presently we went down to the sea and swam in the warm waters until the sun sank and pushed the mountain's shadow over the beach, making it look cold and drained of colour.

## Light Layer Cake

*2oz butter*
*2oz caster sugar*
*4oz plain flour*
*½ tsp baking powder*
*2 eggs*

Work the butter and the sugar to a cream that is quite white. Separate the egg yolks, beat well then mix with the flour and baking powder. Beat the egg whites to a stiff froth and fold them into the rest of the mixture. Turn mixture into an oblong tin and bake in a hot oven for 15 minutes. Turn out and allow to cool before cutting in half horizontally and spreading strawberry jam in the sandwich. Paint with the top with icing sugar solution if desired.

## The Tale of the Turk, the Ram
## and the Chocolate Cake

Gerry had spent a pleasant afternoon drifting up and down the coast in his boat, looking for seals. Returning home, he burst into the drawing room in search of tea and a slice of the mammoth chocolate cake he knew his mother had made. A curious sight met his eyes.

Mother was seated on a cushion, gingerly holding in one hand a piece of rope to which was attached a small, black and excessively high-spirited ram. Sitting around Mother, cross-legged on cushions, were a fierce-looking old man in a tarbush and three heavily veiled women. Also ranged on the floor were lemonade, tea, and plates of biscuits, sandwiches and the chocolate cake. As I entered the room, the old man had leant forward, drawn a huge, heavily ornate dagger from his sash, and cut himself a large hunk of cake which he stuffed into his mouth with every evidence of satisfaction. It looked rather like a scene out of the Arabian Nights.

The context and the results of this unusual tale of afternoon tea is told in 'Dogs, Dormice and Disorder', the first chapter in *The Garden of the Gods*. Here is the recipe for what Gerry referred to as a 'mammoth chocolate cake'.

## Mammoth Chocolate Cake

*6oz Paisley (self-raising) flour*
*6oz caster sugar*
*6oz softened butter*
*3 eggs*
*1½ flat tsp baking powder*
*2 tsp vanilla essence*
*4 tbsp boiling water*
*4oz cocoa powder*

Mix together flour, sugar, butter, eggs and baking powder in a large bowl. In a separate bowl mix the cocoa powder with the boiling water, adding the water a little at a time and stirring to make a stiff paste. Add this to the cake mixture and combine well. Spoon the mixture into two greased baking tins lined with greaseproof paper, and flatten top. Bake in a medium oven for 20 to 25 minutes. Leave to cool in the tin, then turn out on to a wire rack to cool completely. Place one cake on top of the other and use jam, whipped cream or chocolate to stick together.

## *Soojee/Semolina Sweets*

That Louisa made good use of her copy of *Bengal Sweets* by Mrs J. Haldar is implicit in its well-thumbed, stained and greased pages, but nevertheless, some detective sleuthing is required to find the clues that suggest the most popular recipes. The most popular appear to have been those based on the use of semolina, or *sujji*, *soojie* or *soojee* in various Hindi transliterations, the coarser grains, or wheat middlings, formed in flour-making and commonly used today in the manufacture of pasta and couscous. The actual word semolina is derived from the Italian word *semola*, meaning bran, in turn derived from the Latin *simila* and originally from the Greek *semidalis*, meaning groats. In British culture, especially that of school dinners, semolina has come to mean a sloppy mixture of semolina wheat mixed with milk and served as a dessert.

Bearing this penchant for soojee/semolina sweets in mind, the book is marked at pages 72–73 by the insertion of a detached last page (page 131–132), which features a Conclusion and Tables of Weights and Measures. A spent matchstick is stuck in the binding, suggesting that either Louisa was smoking a cigarette whilst consulting the recipes, or had just lit the charcoal fire. We will reproduce two of the recipes on these two marked pages on the assumption that they were amongst the family favourites, if only in the 1920s when Gerry was a young child.

# Magadh Ladoo (Sweet Semolina Balls)

*1lb soojee*
*14oz ghee (or melted butter)*
*1lb 4oz sugar*
*cardamom major*
*raisins*

Take the ghee in a pan and melt it over a gentle fire. Throw in sujji and stew it stirring constantly. The grains of soojee will swell considerably by absorbing the ghee and assume a fawn colour. Then it is properly cooked for the subsequent operation. Pour out the fried soojee on a plate and mix in the sugar well. Strew over cardamom seeds and raisins and heap up the mass. Nothing now remains to be done save to make out balls from it but the whole difficulty lies there. The ghee is generally taken in a little excess and it oozes out from soojee when poured on the plate. Now when sugar is mixed it dissolves in the surplus ghee, gets sticky and serves as the only binding agent on drying. To work satisfactorily take from the mixture of sujji and sugar a little at a time; blend the two ingredients well and mould into round balls applying gentle pressure with the fist. The balls will retain their shape without crumbling if they are formed whilst the mass is warm.

'Cardamon major' are fruits of the large cardamom (*Amomum subulatum*) in which each capsule has many seeds and a single fruit may suffice for the recipe. The seeds of the common cardamom (*Elettaria cardamomum*) are an acceptable substitute.

Soojee Biscuits are just about as simple and plain as biscuits can be.

## Soojee Biscuits

Mix 1lb soojee, 4oz butter, 1oz sugar a small teaspoon salt, and milk sufficient to make a soft dough. Leave it covered in a basin for four hours, then knead it on a floured board, roll out quarter of an inch thick, cut in rounds, prick and bake.

Louisa also had simple recipes for a number of dainty desserts which she usually served cold in small ramekin-sized dishes. Here are two samples. In the second, she used either semolina or cornflour, her personal taste deciding the latter is preferable.

## Semolina Pudding

*2oz semolina*
*1 pint milk*
*1oz caster sugar*
*1 egg*
*lemon peel*

Mix the semolina with a little milk in a bowl. In a pan, boil the rest of the milk with a few strips of lemon peel and when it boils, remove the peel and stir in the semolina. Add the sugar and boil gently for five minutes. Allow the mixture to cool slightly and stir in one well beaten egg. Pour into a buttered pudding–dish and bake in a gentle oven until set. Sprinkle with nutmeg or cinnamon and serve hot or cold.

## Lemon Blancmange

*2 cups water*
*2 tbsp cornflour*
*one lemon*
*whites of two eggs*
*4oz sugar to taste*

Pour water into an enamel saucepan and set it to boil with the rind of the lemon. When boiling add cornflour mixed with a little cold water. Boil for a few minutes then add sugar and lemon juice. Beat the egg whites to a stiff froth, add to mixture and beat well. Pour into individual bowls and allow to cool in the icebox before serving.

## Scones, Rock Cakes, and the Perpetuation of Englishness

Perhaps nothing could be a more English and Anglo-Indian practice than taking tea and scones, in whichever way one chooses to pronounce the name of the sweet afternoon staple. Gerry always ate SCONNS, never SCOANS, with strawberry preserve and clotted cream. The family tradition in Corfu had a lifelong influence on him and whenever he was in London in later years he would always try to make time for afternoon tea and scones in the Palm Court of the Ritz Hotel, which as the hotel brochure describes, is 'an institution in itself and a quintessential British experience.' He always drank loose-leaf tea, never tea made with bags, but did not have a particular taste for a special Indian blend. The Darjeeling First Flush and Assam Tippy Orthodox at the Palm Court might have attracted his attention, but his choice would not have been connoisseurial. He took his tea with a little milk to produce the dark-coloured suspension which is presently referred to as 'builders' tea' – even in the Indian subcontinent – and his use of sugar varied down the years. He frequently referred to the drink as *cha*, the word commonly used for simple tea in West Bengal, but he never drank the sweet, spicy Indian *chai* of other regions.

In Corfu, whenever Mother asked who was going to be in for tea, there was usually a unanimous response in favour, because it was certain that there would be scones available. There was, however, a requirement that all her children should behave impeccably while she entertained the invited guests. Many are the examples that one might cite, beginning with the invitation of Margo's Turkish boyfriend to whom Spiro had taken such a dislike, a tale which is told in 'The Sweet Spring' chapter of *My Family and Other Animals*.

'I wouldn'ts trust a sonofabitch Turk with any girls. He'll cuts her throats, thats what he'll do. Honest to Gods, Mrs Durrells, its not safe, Missy Margo swimming with hims.'

Mother suggested that Margo bring her new boyfriend to tea and while her daughter delightedly ran off to fetch him, she hastily made a cake and some scones, warning the rest of the family to be on their best behaviour. Their politeness was probably too unctuous as they listened to their supercilious young guest who bragged that he could write superbly if he tried, that he was a superb swimmer, that he rode a horse expertly and that he could sail a boat into a typhoon without fear. The result of the family's polite attention at the tea party was an invitation to Margo and Mother to accompany him to the cinema that evening.

Another example is told in Chapter 4 of *The Garden of the Gods*, 'The Elements of Spring', after Gerry had acquired three baby eagle owls. Having fed them the ten lamb chops that Mother had intended for the family's lunch, Leslie is persuaded to shoot a week's supply of sparrows with his air rifle to sustain the chicks in the forthcoming days.

'I'm making some scones,' said Mother, and sighs of satisfaction ran round the table, for Mother's scones, wearing cloaks of home-made strawberry jam, butter and cream, were a delicacy all of us adored. 'Mrs Vadrudakis is coming to tea so I want you to behave,' Mother went on.

Mother was entertaining Mrs Vadrudakis to tea and scones on the veranda and the topic of conversation was the possibility that they might start a society for the elimination of cruelty to animals, a sort of Corfiot branch of the RSPCA. The two earnest ladies were sitting rather stiffly, clasping cups of tea, surrounded by bloodstained corpses of numerous sparrows as Leslie demonstrated his accuracy of aim. Mother was just smiling nervously at her guest at the very moment a dead sparrow fell into the strawberry jam.

There is a recipe for scones in the 1887 manuscript, but it is barely intelligible in the way it is written, without punctuation or measures for ingredients. Moreover, it uses soojee, and in this respect, it is not a recipe for the type of scone Louisa served at afternoon tea in Corfu. There is, however, one in the handwritten collection from the 1923–35 Dulwich days. It is reproduced below in three forms with different measures for the ingredients that reflect the generations through which it was used by the Dixie-Durrells. We have not converted the quantities to the grams of the modern decimalised day, for nowhere did any of Louisa's recipes use such a system. A little imperial ingenuity will thus be required.

## Scones

*8 ch/2 cups/16oz wheat flour*
*1 ch/¼ cup/2oz sugar*
*1 kach/2 tsps/½ oz baking powder*
*pinch of salt*
*5 kach/⅓ cup/2½ oz unsalted butter*
*1 egg lightly beaten*
*½ kach/1 tsp/⅓ oz vanilla extract*
*2 ch/½ cup/4oz milk*

*(4 kachcha (kach) = 1 chittak (ch) = 2oz)*

Mix the flour, sugar, baking powder and salt in a large bowl; gently rub in small pieces of butter with fingertips to give crumble structure; add milk, egg and vanilla together and then mix into the crumble to form a smooth dough; knead the dough, but gently, into a 7-inch round and then cut out smaller 2½-inch rounds; place on baking sheet and brush tops with milk for glaze. Bake for 15 minutes in a medium oven till the tops are browned and the toothpick test is clean.

The type of teas served up by Louisa in Corfu were essentially based upon the kind of Anglo-Indian afternoon tea she might have presented on the verandas of her bungalows, from Roorkee to Jalalabad, and from Jamshedpur to Lahore. They were essentially a feature of the English influence in India brought back to southern England and then taken on to Corfu. Of a more direct influence in the perpetuation of Englishness in foreign lands was the habit that Nancy Durrell and Pamela Wilkinson – respective wives of Larry and Gerry's first tutor, George – instituted in their villas in Perama in 1935. Theirs was the perspective of experience in London and southern England, with no Indian influence. Joanna Hodgkin writes in *Amateurs in Eden*, Chapter 6, 'Prospero's Island':

> To begin with at least, the novelty of Corfu life was combined with a rather old-fashioned Englishness; Nancy and Pam baked cakes; they enjoyed traditional afternoon teas; they made jams and chutneys. When not occupied swimming, sunning and walking, the women were often to be found in the kitchen . . .

Larry and his companions, Theodore, Zarian and the Count, had spent time discussing the all-but-vanished English culture in Corfu, deciding they would find little more than ginger beer, rock cakes and cricket. The tale was told in the 'History and Conjecture' chapter in Larry's *Prospero's Cell* (16.11.37) how, when the battleships of the British fleet anchored in the harbour, there would inevitably be the spectacle of a cricket match between a naval force and a team made up of local players from the two town clubs. Larry wrote:

> When the news comes that the challenge to a cricket match has been received, there is an audible sigh of relief and pleasure which runs the length of the town. At once a profound clamour of activity breaks out; a matting pitch is laid in the centre of the esplanade; a marquee is hastily run up; and the Ministry of Supply in Athens receives an incoherent telegram asking it to obtain from the British Legation the recipe for rock cakes, which has somehow been mislaid once again this year.

The organisers had no need to go to such lengths; Louisa had a recipe in her collection:

## Rock Cakes

*8oz Paisley (self-raising) flour*
*2 tbsp caster sugar*
*2oz butter*
*1 egg*
*2 tbsp currants*
*milk*

Mix the flour and sugar and rub in the butter. Add the currants and the egg, well beaten, and enough milk to moisten. Butter some bun tins and spoon the mixture into them in rough heaps. Bake for 20 minutes in a quick oven.

## Some Jams and Preserves

There is a general absence of recipes for bread in Louisa's cookbooks and one can but assume that when in India, the task of baking bread fell to the *khansamas*, and when in England and Corfu, fresh bread was bought regularly from local bakeries. Toast and marmalade for breakfast and watercress sandwiches for a picnic are both mentioned in Gerry's writings, but bread and jam does not seem to be mentioned. But, whether as a filling for a cake, spread on scones, or served as a mix for semolina, a liberal application of jam of one sort or another was vital to the Durrellian sweet tooth. When Nancy complained that there was very little fruit available in Corfu for making jam during the winter months of 1935–6, she was almost certainly referring to those fruits which were used for what may be regarded as typically English jams – strawberry, raspberry, blackcurrant, plum and the like. As she remembered, most of her concoctions were variations on the vegetable marrow and tomato theme, not together, but separately and usually in combination with that vital oriental ingredient, ginger (*Zingiber officinale*), a plant thought to have originated in India and to have reached Greece and Italy by the first century AD. There is a recipe in Louisa's collection referred to as 'Marrow and Ginger Jam', probably the recipe which Nancy was instrumental in following. Perhaps the first instruction for all the recipes for jams and marmalades to be made in the Durrell households should have been: 'First, make sure that all wildlife – water snakes, seahorses and the like, have been removed from your preserving pan and that the utensil has been thoroughly cleaned and sterilised!'

## Marrow and Ginger Jam

*2lbs marrow flesh, peeled and deseeded*
*3½ oz peeled root ginger*
*juice of two lemons*
*1 tsp cinnamon*
*2lbs sugar*
*(weights of marrow and sugar should be the same)*

Squeeze lemons into a bowl, then grate marrow flesh and ginger into the same bowl. Mix. Transfer the mixture to a preserving pan, add 1 tsp cinnamon and stir over low heat for 5 minutes or so until the marrow falls and starts to lose juice. Add 2lbs sugar, turn up the heat and boil hard, stirring until it reaches its setting point, 10 minutes, no more than 20 minutes. Scoop off the scum and pour into sterilised jars. Allow to cool before sealing.

A recipe for Fig and Ginger Jam follows much the same procedure.

Louisa also made Quince Jam, the much-loved Greek *Marmalatha Kythoni*, from the fruits of *Cydonia oblonga*, an introduced small tree species, related to the apple and the pear and relatively common in the north of the island. The fruit of all these three trees of the rose family would have been of special interest to Gerry because when they begin to ripen and rot, the rose beetle, which earlier in the year nectars in the flowers of both the wild and garden roses, is attracted by the same chemicals as occur in the flowers, and the beetle often swarms in the trees. Some of the breakdown products are fruit alcohols and the beetles become stupefied and fall to the ground. It was, no doubt, in such a situation that the Rose-Beetle Man collected his specimens. There is, however, no record of Louisa being troubled by rose beetles during her jam-making.

## Quince Jam

*4lbs quince*
*1 cup water*
*4 cups sugar*
*1 tbsp lemon juice*

Peel and core the quince directly into a bowl of water to prevent browning. Drain into a clean pan, cover with fresh water and boil for half an hour. Remove from heat and leave the pot to stand for another half hour. Drain the liquid and set aside for quince jelly and squash the fruit. Transfer the squashed fruit to a preserving pan, add 4 cups of sugar and 1 cup water and bring to the boil, stirring continuously with a wooden spoon. Simmer, still stirring, for 30–40 minutes till the jam gels and the excess water is boiled away. Add 1 tbsp lemon juice, stir in for 5 minutes and remove from heat. Cool for half an hour then transfer to jars to cool longer before sealing.

There is a familiar recipe for Marmalade Jelly in Louisa's Dulwich College loose-leaved manuscript notebook from the 1920s and 1930s, which is one of the easiest to follow in a stepwise recipe, clearly written as illustrated. The use of 'brandied paper' – probably waxed paper soaked in brandy as a preservative sealant – is to prevent subsequent bacterial and fungal growth and impart some form of sterilisation.

## Marmalade Jelly

Take any number of Seville oranges allowing 1 lemon to every 12 oranges. Cut them across, squeeze the juice and pips into a basin, and cut the remainder of the oranges into pieces with a mincing machine. Weigh the fruit together and to every pound put 3 pints of cold water and allow it to stand for 24 hours. Boil the fruit very slowly for at least 6 hours. Then pour the boiled fruit into a strainer cloth or a hair sieve and allow it to drain until next day. Then weigh the juice, add one pound of best loaf sugar for every pint, stir it on the stove until it is dissolved, then boil it more rapidly until it bubbles. Pour the jelly into small jars and lie down with brandied paper.

Perhaps the most unusual of her citrus-preserve recipes, and probably the most appropriate for the time spent in Corfu, is what she calls Tangerine Marmalade. This was probably the home-made marmalade that Gerry records as relishing on his breakfast toast. He refers on several occasions to the tangerine trees in the garden of Villa Anemoyani, under which the family habitually had breakfast, and these trees would surely have been the source of the fruit. The Corfu variety is small – around 40mm in diameter and weighing in at between 24 and 31 grams – and the time when they are harvested for jamming is critical. At their best in December and January, they are pulpy, succulent and full of pectin, but by May they are full of pips and less fleshy. Early in the year they will make marmalade with no problems of setting, but later, when the pectin levels have dropped, the mixture tends not to set and a jelly or coulis is all that can be expected.

## Tangerine Marmalade

*2lb tangerines*
*juice of one lemon*
*2 cups sugar*

Cut tangerines in half and squeeze in a juicer to make 1½ cups; save the peel and flesh. Remove all seeds from the pulp and grate the peel into small pieces. Cover the peel with water in a small pan, bring to the boil and simmer for 5 minutes; drain. Return peel to pan, add pulp and juice, bring to the boil, reduce heat and simmer for 15 minutes. Add 2 cups sugar, boil, then simmer for half an hour, stirring constantly with a wooden spoon. Add juice of one lemon and watch for signs of setting. Spoon into sterilised jars and cool before sealing.

As a tailpiece to this section on citrus preserves, it is worth noting that nowhere in Louisa's archive is there a recipe that makes use of the now prevalent kumquat, which would not have been widely planted in the 1930s.

Marmalade Jelly

Take any number of seville oranges allowing 1 lemon to every 12 oranges. Cut them across, squeeze the juice and pips into a basin. And cut the remainder of the oranges into pieces with a mincing machine.

Weigh the fruit together and to every pound put 3 pints of cold water and allow it to stand for 24 hours. Boil the fruit very slowly for at least six hours. Then pour the boiled fruit into a strainer cloth or a hair sieve and allow it to drain until next day. Then weigh the juice add one pound of best loaf sugar for every pint stir it on the stove until it is dissolved, then boil it more rapidly until it bubbles.

Pour the jelly into small jars & tie down with brandied paper.

Marmalade Jelly: the Epitome of the Durrellian Sweet Tooth

# 8

# Cooking for Larry's
# International Guests

The Daffodil-Yellow Villa in Kondokali. *The Party Villa.*

A feature of many of the tales in *The Corfu Trilogy* involves the interactions of Gerry and the family with the artistic and literary guests that Larry had invited to visit and stay, often to the displeasure of his mother, who inevitably had to help entertain and feed them. Louisa had a reputation for her use of spicy powders and the concoction of a variety of dishes that came to be interpreted under the general head of 'curry', literally any spicy sauced dish that popular culture believed had their origins in the Indian subcontinent. The popular gastronomic perception of the Durrell family household in Corfu was essentially that expressed by Theodore Stephanides when he commented that dinner almost always included a curry, 'as old Mrs Durrell had lived many years in India and was an excellent cook'. A curry of some description was inevitably Louisa's signature dish, her fallback option whenever she entertained guests. But, then again, she was always polite and respectful of the cuisine of her international guests and, partly out of this respect, partly from a personal desire to accept new culinary challenges, she tended to try and cook dishes she imagined would be special for the specific occasion. Here are a few examples.

# Zatopec and Friends

Perhaps the classic example is to be found in that chapter of *My Family and Other Animals*, called 'The Tortoise Hills,' when five unexpected guests turn up in a sequence beginning with Zatopec, an Armenian poet, a prodigious drinker from morning until night. Then, there were the three English artists, Jonquil, Durant and Michael, the former assuring Louisa in her cockney accent that she had not 'come for no bleeding 'oliday,' that she had come to work and was not interested in picnics. She retired almost immediately to sunbathe and sleep in the garden. Finally, Melanie, Countess de Torro, arrived, having just recovered from a bout of erysipelas, and astonished everyone by discarding her scarlet wig to reveal her bald head, apparently a side effect of the disease.

Larry sent an invitation to Theodore to join the party and he arrived in a carriage accompanied by Zatopec, who had caught the wrong boat for Bosnia, ended up in Athens and boarded the next boat back to Corfu, bringing with him several crates of wine. Once Theodore had been consulted by the Countess about her symptoms and he had reassured Louisa that erysipelas was not contagious, he doubtless suggested that since the villa was virtually awash with the plentiful supplies of Zatopec's red wine, she should cater for such an international party with presumed diverse culinary tastes by cooking that most traditional Corfiot dish, *kokkinisto*.

She and Lugaretzia would probably have already pre-empted this suggestion and begun marinating the lamb for this slowly cooked dish, the name of which translates literally as 'reddened', a most suitable epithet for the condition of Melanie, Countess de Torro! Gerry wrote:

> The dinner that night was colourful and extraordinary, and I was so fascinated by the assembly of characters and the various conversations that I did not know which one to listen to with undivided attention. The lamps smoked gently and cast a warm, honey-coloured light over the table, making the china and glass glitter, and setting fire to the red wine as it splashed into the glasses . . . The plates of food, piled like volcanoes steaming gently; the early fruit in a polished pile in the centre dish; Lugaretzia hobbling round the table, groaning gently to herself; Theodore's beard twinkling in the lamplight; Leslie carefully manufacturing bread pellets to shoot at a moth that hovered around the lamps; Mother, ladling out food, smiling vaguely at everyone . . .

There is a recipe in Louisa's papers, probably collected from Lugaretzia, which correctly uses lamb and both the red wine and tomatoes as the colouring agents. We have given the name Kokkinisto Lamb Zatopec to this variant of the common dish in honour of the provider of the red wine, the use of which was a relatively uncommon occurrence in Louisa's culinary experience. The country bread, mentioned in the recipe below, which Leslie was treating with such disdain, would have been the peasant cornbread, made from maize flour and the 'early fruit' mentioned in the above extract would have been melons, watermelons, peaches, oranges and perhaps cherries or green figs.

## Kokkinisto Lamb Zatopec

Take 2½ lbs of lamb (leg steaks or neck fillets) chopped into chunks, rubbed with salt, and marinade overnight in half a bottle red wine with two bay leaves. Remove lamb in the morning and reserve wine liquor. Heat 3 to 4 tbsp olive oil, add lamb and fry quickly till glazed brown, stirring as necessary. Remove meat, reduce heat and fry three chopped onions, two chopped garlic cloves in meat juice until onions become transparent. Then add marinating liquor, two large tomatoes (chopped), two bay leaves, a pinch of oregano, a pinch of cinnamon and three cloves, salt and pepper to taste. Return lamb to pan, add ½ pint water and bring to the boil. Reduce heat and simmer for 1½ hours or until meat is tender, adding water as necessary to prevent boiling dry. Leave to stand overnight, reheat the following day and serve in the evening with rough country bread and boiled rice to soak up the sauce.

Then, there were many more of Larry's artistic acquaintances, all of whom seemed to present new and exciting challenges to Louisa's culinary repertoire.

## Cooking with Sven

Gerry relates the story of the arrival of the Swedish sculptor, Sven Olson, at the Daffodil-Yellow Villa in Kontokali, in 'The Pygmy Jungle' chapter of *Birds, Beasts and Relatives*, and how, at his welcome he smiled lovingly at Mother and then coughed violently after swallowing a piece of toast, assuring the onlookers that toast always had that effect on him. He tells of the visitor's constant desire to play his accordion, his apparently inexhaustible repertoire, and his insistence of marching round the table at mealtimes playing tuneless Scottish reels. By the time Sven had been in residence for three days, the family had become more or less inured to his playing and had begun to find him quite charming. Gerry wrote:

He exuded a sort of innocent goodness, so that whatever he did one could not be annoyed with him, any more than you can be annoyed with a baby for wetting its nappy. He quickly endeared himself to Mother, for, she discovered, he was an ardent cook himself and carried round an enormous leather-bound notebook in which he jotted down recipes. He and Mother spent hours in the kitchen, teaching each other how to cook their favourite

dishes, and the results were meals of such bulk and splen-
dour that all of us began to feel liverish and out of sorts.

The nature of Louisa and Sven's liaisons in the kitchen will
never be known, for access to Sven's enormous notebook is
not possible; there remain merely a few scribbled scraps,
annotated in two distinct hands, which tend to suggest that
one of the topics of culinary conversation and comparison
was the relative importance of rice in the Indian, Corfiot and
Nordic cuisines. There are certain recipes in Louisa's collection which could conceivably be considered to have a Swedish
equivalent and with reference to what might be construed as
a modern equivalent of Sven's notebook, namely Magnus
Nilsson's magnum opus, *The Nordic Cookbook (2015)*, it is
possible to suggest some of the comparative conversations
between Louisa and Sven. Take, for example, perhaps the
most common worldwide sweet rice dish with variations in
English, Indian, Greek and Swedish – in four of its forms,
respectively, Rice Pudding or Porridge/*Kheer*/*Rizogalo*/
*Risgryngröt*. Louisa's recipe was basically a Greek *rizogalo* modification of her Indian *kheer* recipe, using short-grain *arborio*
rice, as opposed to long-grain basmati rice.

## Rice Pudding

*1 cup (8oz) short-grain rice*
*1½ pints (800ml) milk*

*a good pinch of salt*
*1 stick of cassia cinnamon*
*6 green cardamoms*

Boil the rice in ¾ pint (400ml) salted water over medium heat, stirring constantly. Drain and set aside. Allow the milk to come to the boil gently; reduce the heat and add the rice, cinnamon stick and cardamoms, simmering for another half an hour and stirring occasionally. Adjust consistency with a little more milk if too thick, remove cinnamon stick and sprinkle with sugar to taste for desired sweetness.

*Cinnamomum cassia* is an evergreen tree originating in China but widely planted in India and used predominantly in Indian cuisine. Its bark is hard, unlike that of Ceylon cinnamon (*C. verum*), which crumbles easily in the hand.

In the form of *risgryngröt*, rice porridge is apparently eaten all the year round in Sweden, but especially at Christmas when it is common practice to hide an almond in the dish. The person finding it in his or her portion receives an 'almond gift', usually a piece of confectionery and, according to folk-lore, the find foretells that the person will get married within the forthcoming year. Perhaps the belief would foretell of a romance between the collaborating cooks!

Indian stuffed cabbage rolls are predominantly vegetarian in nature and the pork or other meat is often replaced with paneer. Moreover, not only are common cabbage (*gobhee* –

*Brassica oleracea*) leaves stuffed, but also those of *cheenee gobhee* (Chinese cabbage – *Brassica rapa*). Louisa's recipe for Greek *lahanodolmades* is given below. It is interesting to note that the second part of the Swedish name for this dish – *dolme* – is the equivalent of the Greek dolma, as expressed in dolmades, the parcels of meat and rice, wrapped with vine leaves rather than cabbage (*kål*). Many Swedes would consider this to be an iconic dish of their country.

## Pork Mince and Rice Cabbage Rolls/ Bandh Gobhee Rolls/ Lahanodolmades/Kåldolme

Take 4oz cold rice pudding and several outer leaves of cabbage (preferably stout winter leaves). Bring a large pot of water to the boil and boil the detached cabbage leaves individually, then set aside to cool. Fry 2 finely chopped spring onions in a little olive oil and cool. For the filling, mix the onions with 12oz minced pork, two eggs, a teaspoon of parsley and another of dill, and salt and white pepper to taste. Spread out a cabbage leaf on a chopping board and place a spoonful of the filling in the middle of the leaf. Fold the edges of the leaf inwards and roll into a dolma shape. Repeat for all the leaves and place them seam side down in an ovenproof dish. Add 1 tbsp olive oil and cook for 10 minutes. Pour 2 cups (500ml) of reserved cooked cabbage liquid into the dish and return to the medium hot oven to cook for another 10–15 minutes. Serve with mashed potatoes.

It seems hard to believe that salted cod was just as readily available in India and Corfu and throughout the Mediterranean region as in Scandinavia, the region closest to its major fishing grounds of the North Atlantic Ocean. In Corfu it could be found on sale in even the small village shops. In *Amateurs in Eden*, for example, Nancy's daughter, Joanna Hodgkin, writes from her mother's notes, first, about the walk from Kalami to the shrine of St Arsenius; and then:

> A short walk in the other direction brought them to Kouloura with its little shop selling matches, paraffin, hard cheese and salted cod, but not much else.

This suggests that salted cod was an essential staple of many a household. The following recipe is for the Greek *bakaliáros plaki*, from Corfu, which like all the others, insists that the salted cod should be soaked in a bucket of water for at least twenty-four hours, changing the water three or four times. Louisa's version would appear to be distinct in that it includes the three herb ingredients of her favourite bouquet garni – parsley, thyme and bay leaf – used at different stages of the process of cooking.

## Baked Salted Cod/Kadda Maccha Jhola/ Bakaliáros plaki (Klassisk klippfisk) all with potatoes

Chop 2 onions and place in the bottom of a casserole dish and sprinkle with 2 to 3 tbsp chopped parsley. Fry 2 cloves of crushed garlic and one finely chopped red chilli in 2 tbsp olive oil in a separate pot and add 4 chopped tomatoes, sprigs of thyme, 2 bay leaves and salt and pepper to taste. Cook for 30 minutes then remove the bay leaves. Chop a large piece of cod into 3-inch pieces and lay on the parsley. Peel and slice 2½ lbs potatoes and lay on the fish. Pour the sauce over the potatoes. Then add one cup of water, place the dish on a tray and bake in a medium-hot oven for an hour and a half.

The use of anchovies would more than likely have been a major topic in the comparisons of Louisa and Sven and the use of the readily available fresh Mediterranean anchovies (*gavros*) in combination with free-range eggs from Louisa's flock would probably have been a delightful opportunity for the Swede. The Scandinavian egg-and-anchovy salad (*gubbröra*) was really only different from the Corfiot *gavros kai ta avgá saláta* (below) in its use of fresh specimens of the fish. In translation from Swedish, *gubbröra* means 'Old Man's Mess', and the recipe usually relied on tinned sprats (*skarpsill* or brisling). Louisa also sometimes used her own marinated anchovies preserved in jars. In Bengal she would have preserved the larger Indian anchovy (*Stolephorus indicus* – *phasa* in Bengali), a species in the same family of fish as the European anchovy (*Engraulis encrasicolus*).

## Egg and Anchovy Salad

*4 eggs*
*8oz fresh anchovies*
*1 spring onion chopped*
*3 tbsp sour cream*
*3 tbsp chopped dill*
*3 tbsp chopped chives*
*white pepper*
*salad for garnish*

Hard boil the eggs, cool rapidly, remove shells and chop. Mix eggs, sour cream, chives, dill and pepper to taste. Top and tail the anchovies, fry gently in lightly salted olive oil and chop with a pair of scissors. Mix anchovies and eggs and spread the mixture on rye bread. Toast lightly under the grill and then cut into fingers. Garnish with small-leaf salad such as rocket or cress and serve with a glass of ouzo.

These were the simple culinary liaisons that so endeared Sven to Louisa, rather than the endless accordion recitals. In truly mischievous fashion, Gerry recorded his departure from the Daffodil-Yellow Villa:

> The cab arrived to take him down to the docks and he embraced each one of us fondly, his eyes full of tears. He climbed into the back of the cab with his Gladstone bag beside him and his precious accordion on his lap and waved to us extravagantly as the cab disappeared down the drive.
>
> 'Such a manly man,' said Mother with satisfaction, as we went inside. 'Quite one of the old school.'
>
> 'You should have told him that,' said Larry, stretching himself out on the sofa and picking up his book. 'There's nothing homos like better than to be told they are virile and manly.'
>
> 'Whatever do you mean?' asked mother, putting on her spectacles and glaring at Larry suspiciously.

## Oven-Roast Flamingo-Chicken for Lumy Lover and Harry Honey

The circumstances surrounding the creation of the dish Aromatic Oven-Roast Flamingo-Chicken with Champagne were a practical joke, played by Leslie and Gerry on two of Larry's guests, Lumis Bean and Harry Honey, a pair of American artists who were passionately devoted to their work. It was not long before they came to be nicknamed Lumy

Lover and Harry Honey, on account of what Gerry referred to as their 'charming naïveté and earnestness' and the endearing way in which they addressed each other. Oh, and they wore far too many bits of gold bling and far too much perfume and hair cream, certainly for Leslie's liking. They were viewed as the ideal subjects for a series of practical jokes, initiated by Leslie with the compliance of Gerry, who reported the various outcomes to Theodore every Thursday. Gerry relates the pranks in 'Ghosts and Spiders', Chapter 2 in *The Garden of the Gods*.

The occasion arose when Leslie introduced the notion that great flocks of flamingos were to be seen on the island and Lumy Lover enthusiastically declared they were his favourite bird and that he would just have to see them. The spoof developed as Leslie made what he called a flamingo decoy from the carcass of a plucked chicken and an old cow's horn he had used for powder for one of his muzzle-loaders. The horn made a sound which Gerry described as being 'somewhere between a foghorn and a raspberry.' He reluctantly lent Leslie some pink flamingo feathers from his collection, the reason for which he was not quite sure, and at ten o'clock the two brothers set out for Lake Chalikiopoulos with Lumy and Harry dressed for flamingo hunting in straw hats and gumboots as prescribed by Leslie. To cut a long story short, the two gullible American flamingo hunters were apprehended by the Durrells' favourite policeman, Filomina Kontakosa, who insisted on inspecting the suspicious-looking bag Harry Honey had in his possession.

He wrestled briefly with the straps of the bag, opened it and handed it to Filomina. The policeman peered into it, gave a triumphant grunt, and pulled from the interior the plucked and headless body of a chicken to which were adhering numerous bright pink feathers. Both the stalwart flamingo hunters went white with emotion.

Harry and Lumy were arrested, taken to the police station and allowed to send a note for Larry to help with their extrication. He ranted at Filomina who realised he had been the butt of a practical joke; shouted at his 'half-witted brothers' and took the American flamingo hunters – and apparently also the headless chicken – back to the villa. Lumy and Harry accepted that it was as much the fault of their high spirits and went back into town to buy a crate of champagne. Filomina was invited up to the villa to sing Greek love songs while they all sat on the terrace, drank champagne and ate the headless chicken which, of course, Mother Louisa could not allow to go to waste. Here is her classic Greek recipe for Oven-Roast Chicken with Potatoes (*Kotopoulo sto fourno me patates*), relatively plain fare with but a few ingredients, yet given a tantalising aroma by the use of oregano and the parsley, bay leaf and thyme of a bouquet garni.

With the champagne, toast '*Filomina kai Foinikopteros*' ('Filomina and the Flamingoes').

## Oven-Roast Chicken with Potatoes

*1 chicken, plucked, dressed and drawn*
*½ cup white wine*
*4 potatoes, peeled and chopped into large cubes*
*small bunch of scallions*
*4 garlic cloves*
*3–4 tbsp olive oil*
*2 tsp oregano*
*bay leaves*
*bouquet garni*
*1 lemon*
*salt and freshly ground pepper*

Dry the chicken then rub with olive oil and season well with salt and pepper. Squeeze half the lemon over the bird and place it in the cavity with scallions and bouquet garni. Sprinkle the bird with oregano, pour wine into casserole, cover with lid and roast for 40 mins. Remove casserole from oven and arrange potatoes, garlic and bay leaves around, moistening with more lemon juice and oil if necessary. Roast for another 40 mins or until potatoes are fork-tender. Remove casserole lid and cook for 5–10 mins to crisp chicken skin.

# A Shrimp Soufflé for Count Rossignol

If ever there was a favourite tale in *The Garden of the Gods*, it would probably be in its eponymous chapter, Chapter 3, which contains an account of the insufferable French Count Rossignol, an acquaintance of an acquaintance, neither of whom Larry had met. Louisa complained bitterly and admonished her son that she could not tolerate complete strangers being sent by complete strangers as if she were running a hotel. Nevertheless, the family awaited his arrival in calm anticipation.

He arrived, unfortunately, in time for lunch, and by the end of the meal, without really trying, he had succeeded in alienating everybody including the dogs. It was, in its way, quite a tour de force to be able to irritate five people of such different character apparently without even being aware of doing so, inside two hours of arrival. During the course of lunch, he said, having just eaten a soufflé as delicate as a cloud in which were embedded the pale pink bodies of freshly caught shrimps, that it was obvious that Mother's chef was not French. Having discovered that Mother was the chef, he showed no embarrassment but merely said that she would then be glad of his presence for it would enable him to give her some guidance in the culinary arts.

Louisa had several soufflé recipes in her cookbooks: cheese soufflé and shrimp soufflé, the main savouries; and sweet puddings like chocolate, semolina, rice, prune, and Swiss soufflés, the latter differing in its requirement of vanilla essence. Here is her recipe for shrimp soufflé.

## Shrimp Soufflé

Take 4oz cold, boiled, dressed shrimps and mix with 4oz breadcrumbs, a pinch of chopped parsley and salt and pepper to taste. Separate the yolk of an egg from the white, beat well and add to the shrimp mixture. Moisten with a little milk. Beat the egg white until stiff and frothy and fold into the mixture. Turn into a greased mould and stand in a bowl of cold water. Cover with greaseproof paper and bake in a middling oven until the soufflé is well risen. Serve with a parsley sauce.

The shrimps would probably have been caught by Gerry himself on one of his favourite hunting grounds along the western shore of Lake Chalikiopoulos, the Chessboard Fields, about which he wrote: 'Here, if you felt hungry, you could wade out into the shallows and catch fat, transparent shrimps that tasted as sweet as grapes when eaten raw.' The shrimps in question would have been the common or brown shrimp (*Crangon crangon*), a familiar crustacean to be found in the pots and on the plates of the shops and restaurants of the

Atlantic and Mediterranean coasts. It turns from brown to a delicate pinky-orange colour when boiled. It is common in shallow, brackish waters in which it lies buried in sand during the day to escape the attentions of predatory birds and fish, and feeds nocturnally.

Entertaining the supercilious Count became a chore, especially for Larry, whom Louisa had insisted should shoulder the burden for the duration of his stay. After he had given the Count a tour of the library and museum in town, the Kaiser's summer palace at Achilleion and taken him to the top of Mount Pantocrator, all of which he considered to pale into insignificance against what one might find in France, it was decided that Gerry should take him out in his boat, the *Bootle Bumtrinket*. Leslie remembered that there was going to be a fish-drive on Lake Chalikiopoulos and eventually Gerry agreed, after bribes from his siblings, to show the Count the habitat from which the shrimps in his soufflé had been gathered.

> The Count outfitted himself in pale blue linen trousers, elegant chestnut-bright shoes, a white silk shirt with a blue and gold cravat knotted carelessly at the throat, and an elegant yachting cap.

He started to complain about the heat as soon as he saw Gerry's homemade boat, mopping his face and moustache with a scent-drenched handkerchief. He complained about the smell of the stagnant waters of the former salt pans, commenting that, 'In France ze water ees hygiene.' Suddenly, Gerry realised that he had not replaced the bung in the drain hole in the bottom of the boat on the last occasion he had used it and slowly he watched the water swirling in and up over the Count's shoes. The Count realised that his precious footwear was being flooded, stood up, rocked the boat and fell into the muddy water amongst the fringing reeds. Gerry got a fit of giggles when the Count swore – '*Merde!*' – but at least Gerry knew he was keeping his mouth above water.

Eventually the Count was extricated and the two walked home, bedraggled and drying in the sunshine, to arrive at the same time as Spiro drew up in his Dodge, bringing the rest of the family home, flushed with wine, in celebration of their temporary break from the nauseous Count. Now he let forth a tirade of abuse, calling Gerry an assassin and ranting on until Larry put his arm around his muddy shoulders and led him off for a brandy and a bath. Unfortunately, the mishap did not have the desired effect that everyone had hoped for.

The Count stayed on grimly, as if to punish us all, and was twice as offensive as before.

Thereafter, there was always an association of the Count with shrimp soufflé and for Gerry, the wider use of the French expletive the Count had unwittingly taught him. *Merde!*

Reception Party on the Veranda of the Daffodil-Yellow Villa.
(Left–right: Margo, Nancy, Larry, Gerry and Louisa).

# 9

# Cooking the Catch
# and Roasting the Bag

Spiro and Gerry Spit-Roasting Snipe for Lunch
at the Lake of the Lilies

The two elder Durrell Brothers – Lawrence (Larry) and Leslie – could hardly have been more dissimilar in character and intellect. Larry was in the process of becoming a writer of international repute and he and his wife, Nancy, were restless in Corfu Town in the early months of 1937, at the time when *Panic Spring*, Larry's second book, was published in London. On 29 April 1937, Larry wrote in *Prospero's Cell*:

It is April and we have taken an old fisherman's house in the extreme north of the island – Kalamai. Ten sea-miles from the town, and some thirty kilometres by road, it offers all the charms of seclusion . . . This is become our unregretted home. A world. Corcyra.

On 5 May, Larry made a cautionary note that they were dependent upon the arrival of a daily caique boat from Corfu Town for their provisions. There was, however, the bountiful sea which lapped upon the rocks on which their house, soon to become known as the White House, stood solidly. Their landlords were a fisherman, Athenaios (Totsa), and his wife Eleni, who, rather confusingly, Larry calls Anastasius and

Helen. It was from Anastasius that Larry learned many of the local techniques of fishing and it was in the shared kitchen at the White House that Nancy was introduced to the traditional recipes by Eleni.

As far as may be judged from references in *The Corfu Trilogy*, Leslie was more than happy to remain in the fold of the family and to eat whatever meal his mother set on the table in front of him. His main interest was in guns and the hunting and shooting of the wild birds and beasts of the island and the neighbouring mainland of Albania and Epirus. Here are a selection of dishes and recipes generated by the brothers which exemplify their integration with different sections of Corfiot society and its different aspects of heritage and tradition.

## *Kalami Kakavia –*
## *Corfiot Fish Stew*

As has been mentioned in Chapter 3 of this book, Larry became troubled with frequent bouts of dyspepsia caused by his sedentary working life and his mother's rich cooking. Yet, according to Theodore Stephanides in his reminiscences published as *Autumn Gleanings* (2011), Larry was very much a bon viveur where food and wine were concerned.

> Lawrence Durrell always enjoyed good food, and here he
> was lucky in having Nancy who was a real cordon bleu

and who could turn out any kind of dish, whether English or Greek, with the most rudimentary materials and utensils. He was not a 'finicky' eater, but the food had to be good; and he could content himself with a local peasant wine, but that, too, had to be of good quality. He soon established himself as the possessor of a discriminating palate among the local peasantry, with the result that their best wine was always reserved for him.

Larry's Chapter IX ('Appendix for Travellers') in *Prospero's Cell* (1945) includes a section entitled 'Dishes to Experiment With', the implication being that he had dined out on such fare when living in Corfu Town. He lists fourteen dishes, eight of which are either fish- or shellfish-based, suggesting a bias to the fruits of the sea in which he and Nancy spent so much time. The species in these dishes were primarily for the traveller, to be ordered and tried in the restaurants in town. The local island fishermen generally netted smaller fish for a staple fish stew. Writing about the diet of Larry and her mother Nancy while they were living in Kalami, Joanna Hodgkin in *Amateurs in Eden* revealed that:

For the most part they ate the same food as the villagers. Apart from greyish-brown bread and macaroni, the staple diet was some kind of fish stew made from small fish cooked with carrots, potatoes, onions and garlic. In the evenings, Totsa and his family and the other villagers often joined them for talk and singing, and Eleni handed

round little cups of Turkish coffee and glasses of ouzo
while Nancy offered biscuits or sweets from a tin.

Small boats plied in and out of the harbours at Kalami and
Kouloura, fishing for a variety of small species as well as
larger fish, like scorpionfish and grey mullet, and octopuses.
Nancy and Larry had a primary food source on their door-
step, and Larry was taught how to cast the shoulder net by
Anastasius, aka Totsa. Larry noted that the net had a span
of about six feet and was loaded with lead on its edges. It
was carried folded on the left shoulder, from where it could
be thrown in a special way to trap shoals of small fish. The
main target fish, the basis of the stew, was *bogue* or *gopa*, a
small member of the sea-bream family, ubiquitous and
common in the coastal waters of the Mediterranean Sea,
notably along the west coast of Greece in the Ionian Sea.
Its Latin name is one of the most ridiculous imaginable. It
was the greatest taxonomist of all time, Carl Linnaeus, who
first described the fish for science and gave it the most
implausible Latin name of *Boops boops*, with no obvious
reason for its scientific origin in anything but the interpretation of the silent mouthing of the fish in an aquarium.
'Boops, boops!' It was probably just one of several idiosyn-
cratic moments the eminent Swede allowed himself in the
never-ending stream of new species that came his way in
need of a classificatory name. Spiro was able to buy *bogue*
in the Corfu fish market. The following recipe is from
Louisa's collection, but as it was probably contributed by

Nancy and Larry, we have called it *Kalami Kakavia*, or Corfiot Fish Stew. A *kakavia* is actually a three-legged cooking pot.

## Kalami Kakavia,
## or Corfiot Fish Stew

Pour 1 cup olive oil into a large cooking pot. Add 6 small peeled potatoes, 2 carrots cut into 1-inch discs, 1 whole medium onion, 1 small tomato (whole), 2 cloves garlic and 1 bay leaf and fry gently, stirring all the time. Pour 8 cups of water into the pot and bring to boil over medium heat. Add 5lbs gutted and scaled *gopa* (or any other small fish or squid will do) and boil for 20–25 minutes. Add juice of 3 lemons five minutes before the end of cooking time. Drain the fish and vegetables from the stewpot and serve on a large platter. Pour the soup into a tureen and serve into individual bowls with plain boiled macaroni.

It seems to have been mainly *gopa* that Margo ate during her dietary days, when she listed the elements of her diet for Larry as possible antidotes for his dyspepsia in Chapter 6, 'The Sweet Spring' in *My Family and Other Animals*:

. . . you could try the orange-juice-and-salad one; that's awfully good. There's the milk-and-raw-vegetable one

. . . that's good too, but it takes a little time. Or there's the boiled-fish-and-brown-bread one.

In one sense, she was taking a Corfiot staple and modifying it to suit her dietary lifestyle.

## *Eleni & Nancy's Ochtapodi Stifado and Eel-Meat in Red Sauce*

Not only did Anastasius teach Larry how to fish with a shoulder net, but he also taught him how to use a trident and an octopus hook when the pair went night-fishing with carbide lamps. Theo Stephanides observed Larry's feelings for cephalopods.

> Squids and octopuses always exercised a great repulsion-fascination for Lawrence, and he rarely refused the opportunity of going on an octopus hunt, whether by day or by night with a carbide lamp, with any of the local fishermen.

Larry has a delightful description of one such event in 'Ionian Profiles', Chapter III in *Prospero's Cell*. The detail of how he and Anastasius speared a scorpionfish with a trident and then caught an octopus with a hooked staff is there for all to read, including the peripheral detail of the ploys used, like scattering a few drops of olive oil with an almond twig to clear the surface water, or the trailing sprig of parsley attached to the octopus staff as a lure. Larry identifies the plant as parsley, but in actual fact it is a related species of the parsley family, a variety of asafoetida, probably *Ferulago nodosa* or *Ferula glauca* in this specific instance. The latex exuding from a cut stem of the plant has a strong garlicky, dung-like smell which attracts carnivorous cephalopods like octopuses. To Anastasius, a fish was a fish, but squid and octopus were delicacies. Back in the White House kitchen, Eleni would probably have kept Nancy under close scrutiny as she cooked *Ochtapodi Stifado*.

## Ochtapodi Stifado

*1 octopus rinsed, cleaned and skinned, eyes and beak removed*

*handful of small onions (kokkari)*

*2 fresh tomatoes, chopped*

*4 fresh pimientos (grown in Nancy's window box)*

*3 garlic cloves*

*½ cup red wine*

*1 cup of olive oil*

*½ tsp sugar*

*2 tbsp tomato paste*

*2 sprigs rosemary*

*oregano*

*2 bay leaves*

*salt and pepper to taste*

Boil octopus for 20 mins in one cup water plus vinegar; remove and chop into pieces and leave in pot with cup of stock. Sauté other ingredients in olive oil for 10 mins, then add to pot with octopus and stock. Add red wine, herbs, sugar, salt and pepper, and bring to boil. Reduce heat and simmer for 40–60 minutes. Serve with macaroni or coarse country bread.

To Larry, fishing was more than the simple acquisition of food for the table. On 7 August 1937 he wrote, 'Fishing demands the philosophic attitude', no doubt inspired by conversations with his friends from the literary circle at the Sign of the Partridge, notably Ivan Zarian and Theodore Stephanides, whom Larry considered to be of almost mythological quality. The three men talked of the ancient Greek philosophers and debated such questions as 'If you had an opportunity to put a question to Socrates what would it be?' Then the discussion drifted to another famous philosopher – Aristotle. Amongst his talents was the ability to distinguish and name most species of fish – he was an excellent ichthyologist – and both Stephanides and Zarian considered that Larry had begun to develop these same Aristotelean attributes. He had even begun to dress like a fisherman in the heavy knitted sweaters sent by his mother. Incidentally, in the Jersey Archives of Louisa Durrell, there are handwritten knitting patterns for a Fisherman's Cap of the type favoured by Larry and depicted on his bust in the Bosketto Gardens, Corfu; and other patterns include a Roll-Neck Raglan Sweater; Cable-Stitch Raglan Cardigan,

Cap-Sleeve Jumper and Spiral Socks. He clearly dressed to look the part of a sailor, fisherman and ichthyologist.

He became familiar with many species of fish, of diverse shapes and sizes. There was the sole (*glossa*) the most common flatfish; the scorpionfish (*skorpidi*), speared by Anastasius; and the threatening moray eel (*Muraena heleni*). He was particularly fascinated by the diverse members of the sea bream family (*Sparidae, sparos*). One of the two most commonly encountered fish on restaurant menus in the twenty-first century is the gilthead sea bream (*Sparus aurata*), originally known by its Greek name of *Tsipoura*, but latterly by the commercial name of *Orata*, an Italian corruption of its Latin specific name. It is farmed in the Bay of Vathi, Kassiopi, off the north-east coast of the island, by the Corfu Sea Farm Company. The Latin generic name of *Sparus* is derived directly from the Greek *sparos*, a general name for several of the closely related species of sea bream, but specifically, annular sea bream (*Diplodus annularis*). Larry encountered what he referred to as *sparos* when he was out night-fishing with Anastasius.

We move in a concave ripple. Deep rock-surfaces, yellow and green and moving like a human scalp with marine fucus. Fishes, a school, the silver-white of *sparos* dawdle to the entrance of a cave and goggle at us. Each wears a black dapple on the back, and they look, in their surprise, like a row of semiquavers. Then, as if frightened by some purely marine event they disappear with the suddenness of a thrown switch.

Larry's interest in sea creatures as potential sources of food extended way beyond the small fish ingredients of the *kakavia* stew and the cephalopods. He wrote in *Prospero's Cell*, 'Divisions Upon Greek Ground', of the events of the fisherman's holiday on 4 May 1937 when the carcass of a loggerhead turtle (*Caretta caretta*) was washed up on the beach. He expected the locals to make some use of its flesh, but only the dogs were interested in its flippers. That was not the only excitement of the day, for Larry follows up the tale of the turtle with that of the hunting of an enormous eel by Anastasius, Old Father Nicholas and several other villagers with boathooks and tridents. This almost satanic monster was a Mediterranean or Roman moray eel (*Muraena helena*), a solitary and territorial species which feeds on fish, cephalopods and dead animals. Larry missed the opportunity to romanticise the conjecture that it had either been following the dying turtle, or that it had been entranced by Helen, daughter of Anastasius and Eleni. There was anxiety among the villages on account of the fact that the bite of the eel could be dangerous.

> Helen was given a terrific scolding because she was in the
> habit of poking about in the rocks at low tide barefooted.
> 'And if such an animal got you?' Anastasius kept
> repeating. 'And if such an animal got you?'

Larry ends his account with a paragraph comprising a single sentence: 'To-night we shall have eel-meat with red sauce for supper.' Unfortunately, the recipe for this dish did not find its way into the Durrell archives, but there are several to be gleaned from the traditional folk cookery. In the context of the hunt described by Larry, the following recipe might be called Eleni's Eel-Meat in Red Sauce, after Eleni the cook and the specific Latin epithet of the moray eel – *heleni*.

## Eleni's Eel-Meat in Red Sauce

Sauté 1 chopped onion in 2 tbsps olive oil in a stew-pot. Add 2lb eel meat cut into chunks and brown on all sides. Add 2 cups finely chopped tomatoes, 1 tbsp tomato paste and a bay leaf, salt and pepper to taste. Stir to blend with a cup of water and simmer for two hours, topping up water as required. Remove bay leaves and serve with macaroni. NB This is essentially a type of *kokkinisto* which uses water instead of red wine.

# *Roasting the Bag: Spit-Roast and Pot-Roast Game Birds*

And so, on to the activities of Gerry's other brother, Leslie, the hunter, whose fascination with guns and the hunting of wild game for both sport and for the table, found references in several passages in *The Corfu Trilogy*. It was a popular pastime in the 1930s, even though, as noted by Larry Durrell in *Prospero's Cell*, Lake Antiniotissa in the north of the island

and Lake Korission in the south were the only localities that might guarantee a decent bag. The true sportsmen, like Leslie, had to make regular planned trips to the Epirus region of the Greek mainland, or to Albania, where shooting for sport was, and still remains, a popular pastime in the twenty-first century. From Gerry's writings, there can be no doubt that brother Leslie shot primarily for sport, and if a quarry found its way into his mother's kitchen, so much the better. The information is hidden in the pages of *My Family and Other Animals*, Chapters 6 and 16, 'The Sweet Spring' and 'The Lake of the Lilies', but the title of Chapter 12, 'The Woodcock Winter', is also rather a giveaway. As far as can be ascertained, Leslie observed the statutory shooting seasons, however lax, and the birds he shot for the table were restricted as follows.

15 September – 28 February: Woodcock (*Scolopax rusticola*), Turtle Dove (*Streptopelia turtur*), Quail (*Coturnix coturnix*)

15 September – 20 February: Wood Pigeon (*Columba palumbus*)

15 September – 10 February: Common Snipe (*Gallinago gallinago*), Wigeon (*Anas penelope*), Pintail (*Anas acuta*), Garganey (*Anas querquedula*), Shoveler (*Anas clypeata*), Tufted Duck (*Aythya fuligula*)

15 September – 31 January: Pochard (*Aythya ferina*), Gadwall (*Anas streptera*), Teal (*Anas crecca*), Mallard (*Anas platyrhynchos*)

On the morning of the visit to The Lake of the Lilies, correctly Lake Antiniotissa, described in Chapter 16, Gerry and Leslie drew lots to decide where the former would collect pond life while the other went hunting in search of game. Leslie drew the west shore with its canebrakes and reed swamps and had a most successful morning, arriving back at the beach in time for lunch 'with a bulging bag of game, hares damp with blood, partridge and quail, snipe and wood pigeons'. It was not long before Spiro was turning seven fat snipe on an improvised olive-wood spit over the flames of a fire, 'while Margo sprawled elegantly in the sun, picking daintily at a pile of fruit and vegetables', and obviously not engaging with the rest of the party.

Skewered as a kebab was the simplest way in which various members of the extended family obviously felt confident and competent in cooking small game birds, either outdoors, as on the beach of 'The Lake of the Lilies' – 'snipe and quail skewered on an olive-wood spit' – or barbecued over charcoal in the kitchen as the 'woodcock skewered on lengths of bamboo' described in 'The Merriment of Friendship' chapter of *The Garden of the Gods*. A variant of the spit-roast for woodcock is referred to in the 'Owls and Aristocracy' chapter of *Birds, Beasts and Relatives* where, as an entrée at lunch with Countess Mavrodaki, Gerry is served 'beak-skewered roast woodcock' on toast with fried potato wafers, asparagus candles and peas.

Louisa had recipes for these species of small game, most of which had strong influences of Indian cuisine in the use of garlic and cumin, and of honey from the hives in the garden, to satisfy the Durrellian sweet tooth. Her recipe for pot-roast quail with honey and cumin was as follows.

## Pot-Roast Quail
## with Honey and Cumin

Take 6 plucked or skinned quail and paste with 2 tbsp honey and 1 tbsp ground cumin. Sauté in 2 tbsp olive oil and 1 tsp crushed garlic in a shallow pan over charcoal. Transfer to a crock-pot, with 2 tbsp water, salt and pepper to taste and cook for 20 minutes to half an hour, ensuring liquid does not boil away.

Woodcocks in Brandy with Rice seems to have been quite a favourite dish in the winter months when the birds were plentiful on their migration and brandy was on hand as a seasonal warmer.

## Woodcocks in Brandy with Rice

*2 woodcocks*
*½ teacup butter*
*½ teacup brandy*
*1 tbsp flour*
*1 teacup fresh mashed tomato and crushed garlic*
*½ tbsp vinegar*

Heat butter and sauté birds; season with salt and pepper. Scald the brandy in a saucepan and pour over birds into pot. Add 2 tbsp of water and cook for half an hour. Boil 1lb of rice for pilaf, washed and strained. Sprinkle salt and pepper to taste and serve the birds whole on a bed of the rice.

## *Wildfowl and Wild Boar from Epirus and Albania*

Leslie's shooting expeditions to the mainland were usually to the extensive wetlands of Epirus, with the primary objective of bagging a range of species from the duck family, which often congregated together in mixed flocks of both dabbling and diving ducks. The former, which feed on the surface of shallow lagoons, were easier targets and hence the more common species he brought back to Mother's Corfiot kitchens would have been mallard, wigeon, teal, gadwall and garganey. Gerry made notes and sketches as Mother and Margo plucked.

Leslie had returned from a trip to the mainland, loaded with game, and puffed up with pride. He had, he explained to us, pulled off his first left-and-a-right. He had to explain in detail, however, before we grasped the full glory of his action. Apparently, a left-and-a-right in hunting parlance meant to shoot and kill two birds or animals in quick succession, first with your left barrel and then with your right. Standing in the great stone-flagged kitchen, lit by the red glow of the charcoal fires, he explained how the flock of ducks had come over in the wintry dawn, spread out across the sky. With a shrill whistle of wings they had swept overhead, and Leslie had picked out the leader, fired, turned his gun on to the second bird, and fired again with terrific speed, so that when he lowered his smoking barrels the two ducks splashed into the lake almost as one. Gathered in the kitchen, the family listened spellbound to his graphic description. The broad wooden table was piled high with game, Mother and Margo were plucking a brace of ducks for dinner, I was examining the various species and making notes on them in my diary (which was rapidly becoming more bloodstained and feather-covered), and Larry was sitting on a chair, a neat, dead mallard in his lap, stroking its crisp wings and watching as Leslie, up to the waist in an imaginary swamp, for the third time showed us how he achieved his left-and-a-right.

In the 'Merriment of Friendship' chapter of *The Garden of the Gods*, Gerry comments that 'a bank of biscuit-brown chickens and young turkeys was interspersed with wild duck stuffed with wild rice, almonds and sultanas'. Here is Louisa's recipe:

## Oven-Roast Wild Duck
## Stuffed with Rice, Almonds and Sultanas

Pluck and draw the wild duck, reserving the offal (liver, heart and kidneys); score the skin and rub a mixture of crushed garlic and black pepper into it. Baste with olive oil from time to time in a pot-roast over two and a half hours. Meanwhile, simmer the offal in water with an onion and bouquet garni for half an hour; remove the bouquet and reserve the stock. Mix six ounces of uncooked rice with two tablespoons each of crushed almonds and chopped sultanas and cook in the stock for 20 minutes in an open pan to reduce the liquid and form the solid stuffing mixture. Force the stuffing into the cavity of the bird and keep warm. Sprinkle whole almonds and sultanas over the duck and serve.

Louisa also had a lemon balm and honey glaze recipe for wild duck. She used lemon balm (*Melissa officinalis*) in a wide range of recipes, to impart a more delicate flavour than that of lemon juice or zest, for example, to flavour soups, sauces and seafood. It was commonly planted in orchards around the island and a tisane, made from either the fresh or dried leaves, was popular. It was also a favourite plant from which the honey bees could collect nectar; hives were often located in orchards and the honey was almost inevitably flavoured with lemon balm.

## Lemon Balm and Honey
## Glaze for Duck

Mix 3 chopped and crushed lemon balm heads with 2 crushed garlic cloves. Warm 3 tbsp honey in a pan, add 3 tbsp olive oil and balm/garlic mixture and whisk to combine. Make slits in the duck skin and drip in the mixture. Glaze all over with honey using a pastry brush.

There are several references to the consumption of wild boar in *The Corfu Trilogy* and Leslie's prime target on his shooting trips to the mainland was almost always this animal. It had apparently been extinct for quite some time on the island after its natural habitat, the forests of Valonian oak, had gradually been restricted in distribution by the single-minded Venetian policy of planting olive groves throughout the island. There are references in *The Corfu Trilogy* to various members of the Durrell family eating roast wild boar, but there does not seem to be an actual recipe in Louisa's collection, in spite of the fact that Gerry noted 'a haunch of wild boar, sticky with wine and honey marinade, thick with pearls of garlic and round seeds of coriander' on the tables of the Christmas party. He had been privileged to eat wild boar as the main dish of his lunch with Countess Mavrodaki, so sumptuously described in 'Owls and Aristocracy' in *Birds, Beasts and Relatives*. There would seem to be little more to add to his description after he had informed the Countess that it was one of his favourite meats, but could he please have a small helping?

'But, of course you shall,' she said, leaning over the great brown, gravy-glistening haunch and starting to cut thick pink slabs of it. She placed three of these on a plate – obviously under the impression that this was, by anyone's standards, a small portion – and then began to surround them with the accoutrements. There were piles of lovely little golden wild mushrooms, chanterelles, with their delicate, almost winy flavour; tiny marrows stuffed with sour cream and capers; potatoes baked in their skins, neatly split and anointed with butter; carrots red as a frosty winter sun and great tree trunks of white leeks, poached in cream. I surveyed this dish of food and surreptitiously undid the top three buttons of my shorts.

The Countess had two helpings, both identical in size, and then called for a pause, during which she smoked a long thin cheroot and ate salted peanuts, while Gerry undid the rest of the buttons on his shorts!

Spiro Charcoal-grilling Kefalias (Mullet)
for Tea at the Lake of the Lilies

# 10
# Gerry's Hunter–Gatherer Contributions

View over Gerry's Home-range Inshore Ecosystem off Perama
where he Fished with Taki Thanatos and Dived for Giant Clams

Gerry's tales of his observation and collection of specimens of the wildlife of the island had a home-range of three to four miles from the villas at Perama, Criseda and Kontokali. His tousled blonde hair made him an outstanding figure and he soon came to be known and admired by many individuals and families in the vicinity – the workaday farmers and goat-herds on their smallholdings and rocky pastures; the olive millers in their presses; and the fishermen in the lagoons and inshore coastal waters. Many of these local people talked about their livelihoods, gave him gifts, and found him specimens for his collection. In essence, he became a kind of primitive hunter-gatherer, a way of life which was, in many ways, a precursor to his collecting of zoological specimens in later life. Some of his scavenging and gathering experiences in Corfu actually provided food for the kitchen table.

One of Gerry's main hunter-gathering habitats were the shores and shallow waters of Lake Chalikiopoulos, a coastal lagoon connected to the open sea in the 1930s, before the causeway from Kanoni to Perama was constructed during the Second World War. It was not dissimilar to some of the less populated lagoons of Venice and, as such, its resources were exploited at various times during the 400 years when Corfu was a key part of the Venetian Empire. On the western shore of the lagoon were the remains of the salt pans, skilfully managed by the control of sea levels to allow evaporation of sea water and promote the crystallisation of salt. The Venetian salt pans, Gerry's 'Chessboard Fields', had long fallen into disuse, but the locals maintained the tradition and practice of *vallicolture*, from the Italian/Venetian word *vallicoltura*, or lagoon fish breeding and management. It was here that Gerry befriended the convict, Kosti Panopoulos, whilst searching for Old Plop, the European Pond Terrapin (*Emys orbicularis*), and what he referred to as water snakes, but which are correctly known as grass snakes (*Natrix natrix*). Both terrapin and grass snake would have undoubtedly been eaten a few centuries ago.

The other aquatic habitat which yielded specimens, both for Gerry's zoological collection and for the kitchen table, was the inshore marine ecosystem along the island's eastern coast, characterised by its underwater forests of Neptune grass (*Posidonia oceanica*). Gerry fished here with other local fishermen, notably, Spiro Kokino, one of a communal group which fished in the bays of Kontokali, using the netting method described by Gerry in the 'Cuttlefish and Crabs' chapter of *Birds, Beasts and Relatives*. Then, there was Taki Thanatos from Benitses who fished around Mouse Island and that stretch of the coast which Gerry named 'The Bay of Olives' in that chapter of the same book. From both sources, Gerry returned home with some prize specimens for the attention of his mother and Lugaretzia.

## *Charcoal-Grilled Kefalia and Cephalo Bianco*

The main farmed fish of *vallicolture* was always Kefalos/Kefalia, the flathead grey mullet (*Mugil cephalus*), an inshore fish of lagoons and river mouths which can tolerate shallow waters with a range of salinities. It feeds in schools on zooplankton and is easily farmed, managed and harvested by fish drives, in which Gerry regularly participated and brought home specimens for his mother to roast over hot charcoals. They were prominent on one of the tables described in 'The Merriment of Friendship' chapter in *The Garden of the Gods*:

> The kefalia I had brought back from the lake were now browned and charcoal blistered, gleaming in a coating of oil and lemon juice, spattered with jade-green flecks of fennel; they lay in ranks on the huge plates, looking like a flotilla of strange boats tied up in harbour.

On another occasion, the picnic on the beach of the Lake of the Lilies also offered the opportunity to catch grey mullet.

> Spiro, clad only in his underpants and looking like some dark prehistoric man, waddled into the stream that flowed from the lake into the sea and stood knee deep, scowling down into the transparent waters, a trident held at the ready as the shoals of fish flicked around his feet.

The grey mullet can still be seen today in this same locality, at the inlet of Lake Antiniotissa, where they are still farmed as in Venetian times, when it was the traditional species used for the popular Venetian dish *Bourdeto me Cephalo Bianco*. In the name of the dish, *bourdeto* is derived from the Venetian word *brodeto* meaning broth. The fish is cooked in a tomato sauce with onion, garlic and spicy red pepper; let us assume that Spiro's catch was taken back to the villa and cooked by Louisa and Lugaretzia. The first step in the recipe is typical of the Venetian *vallicolture*, using coarse sea salt from the adjacent salt pans; it distinguishes this *bourdeto* from those using other species of fish.

## Bourdeto me Cephalo Bianco

Clean and gut the fish and place in a colander with coarse sea salt for 1–2 hours (whole rather than sliced fish is to be prepared). Remove excess salt, place fish in a casserole, cover with water, add 1 chopped onion and cook for 15 minutes. Remove the onion and discard. Add 4 tbsp chopped red pepper and a cup of olive oil and cook for 10 minutes. Add to the fish and ½ cup lemon juice, plus 2 tbsp tomato paste and ½ tsp cayenne pepper. Cook for 10 more minutes and serve with plain macaroni.

## *Kosti and the Cockles*

Mention has already been made of one of Gerry's favourite hunting grounds along the western shore of Lake Chalikio-poulos, the Chessboard Fields. A most enchanting piece of prose leaves the reader in no doubt that the young tyro was living the role of primitive hunter-gatherer in an environment in which he was not completely comfortable or at ease.

> Here, if you felt hungry, you could wade out into the shallows and catch fat, transparent shrimps that tasted as sweet as grapes when eaten raw, or you could dig down with your toes until you found the ribbed nut-like cockles. Two of these, placed end to end, hinge to hinge, and then twisted sharply in opposite directions, opened each other neatly; the contents, though slightly rubbery, were milky and delicious to eat.

It was here that Gerry encountered Kosti Panopoulos in the company of his vicious pet black-backed gull, Alecko, who was destined to become a part of Gerry's collection. Gerry was in the process of catching two grass snakes when he became aware of Kosti's presence and after preliminary exchanges, Kosti said he was going down to his boat by the sea.

> I said I was making for the sea too, first to wash and secondly to find some cockles to eat.

'I'll walk with you,' he said, rising and stretching. 'I have a basketful of cockles in my boat; you may have some of those if you like.'

Gerry met Alecko, stroked him and did not get the antagonistic reaction that Kosti anticipated from the bird he referred to as a bully and a fat, ugly, biting duck.

The gull at being thus addressed opened one eye and gave a short, harsh yarp, which may have been repudiation or agreement. The man leant down and pulled a big basket from under the seat; it was full to the brim with great fat cockles that chinked musically. We sat in the boat and ate the shell-fish . . .

Inevitably, Kosti gave Alecko to Gerry and offered to meet him regularly to take him fishing for food for the bird and also, no doubt, ensure a regular supply of cockles for the kitchen. The bivalve in question was the lagoon cockle (*Cerastoderma glaucum*) of the Mediterranean region, as opposed to the common cockle (*C. edule*) of the estuaries and inshore marine ecosystems of the eastern Atlantic coasts of Europe. The name 'cockle' is derived from Greek by the following etymological pathway – from Old French *coquille*, Latin *conchylia*, and Greek *konkhylion*, meaning 'little shellfish'. In some instances, the molluscs are simply rinsed, shucked (shelled) and eaten raw with a squeeze of lemon juice. More careful recipes, such as that preferred by Louisa, suggest boiling as a precaution, to cause the shells to open and to discard those which do not oblige. A dressing of white wine, garlic, fennel, lemon zest and juice were used in what she called *Conchiglie St Geraldo*, seemingly her whimsical version of the more familiar *Coquilles St Jacques*!

## Lugaretzia's Soupya and Barbounia Tiganita

In *Prospero's Cell*, one of the 'dishes to experiment with' listed by Larry is 'Cuttlefish with sauce. Ask for soupya.' Whereas Larry was renowned for his fishing expeditions for octopus, it was Gerry who described the ingenious method of fishing for its close relative, the common cuttlefish (*Sepia officinalis*), as used by his fisherman friend, Spiro Kokino. He met Kokino in his rickety little boat in which there was an old kerosene tin containing a cuttlefish, around which was a string tied where its head met its body. He said he was going out to catch more cuttlefish and when Gerry enquired how, Kokino reponded by saying 'With love.'

> I felt it was my duty, as a naturalist, to investigate every
> method of capturing animals, so I asked Kokino whether
> it was possible for me to accompany him. We rowed the
> boat out into the blue bay until she hung over a couple
> of fathoms of crystal clear water. Here Kokino took the
> end of the long string that was attached to the cuttlefish

and tied it carefully round his big toe. Then he picked up the cuttlefish and dropped it over the side of the boat . . . The string trailed gradually over the side of the boat then tautened against Kokino's toe. 'Now,' he said, grinning at me, 'we will see what love can do.'

Eventually, it dawned on Gerry that the cuttlefish on the string attached to Kokino's toe was a female and that she would inevitably attract males of the species. Sure enough, within an hour they had caught five male cuttlefish and Gerry had brought one home for Lugaretzia to cook soupya. Mention of a variation of this dish can be found in the text of *Marrying Off Mother* by Gerald Durrell, when the Durrell siblings are discussing the possible consequences of their mother finding a beau and moving away to live in Athens.

'Well, who would cook for us? Lugaretzia?' [Leslie asked.]
'God forbid!' Larry said, with vehemence.
'Do you remember her cuttlefish soup?' asked Leslie.
'Please don't remind me,' said Margo. 'All those accusing eyes floating there, looking up at you – ugh!'

This passage is surely an exaggerated flight of Gerry's artistic licence because most recipes begin with the instruction to remove the eyes, beak and ink-sac, to avoid a horrible mess. The tentacles are reserved and the head, which is the main part of the animal, skinned to reveal the white flesh.

## Lugaretzia's Cuttlefish Soupya

In the basic Venetian/Corfiot recipe, the sliced meat of the head and the tentacles is sautéed in olive oil with garlic, scallions and parsley for ten minutes. Fish stock, half a cup of white wine, salt and pepper to taste are then added, and the mixture casseroled for a further twenty minutes. The contents are strained and 4oz (100g) of short-grain rice cooked in the liquor until fork-tender, after which the cuttlefish mixture is returned to the dish and served hot.

The fish-stock is made separately using the beak, eyes and skin – but not the ink-sac – of the cuttlefish, and this was undoubtedly the concoction Margo mistook for the actual *soupya*! Gerry of course, used the cuttlebone, the internal shell of the animal, to feed to his caged birds and tortoises as a source of calcium.

Still on the subject of Gerry recording the diverse methods of fishing, he relates a tale of fishing with dynamite, as told to him by the bad-tempered, gnarled old olive-press owner, Papa Demetrios, who amongst other things, popped maize corn cobs for Gerry and gave him a pale pink gecko, the caterpillar of an oleander hawkmoth and a rather large spade-footed toad, which he christened Augustus Tickletummy. The tale was of the mishap of Andreas Papoyakis who blew off his hand while failing to throw a stick of dynamite at a school of *barbounia* in a little bay near the village of Benitses. The penalty for dynamite fishing was five years in prison and a heavy fine, but the police thought Andreas had been punished enough by losing his hand, took pity on him and waived both the prison sentence and fine.

*Barbounia* is red mullet (*Mullus barbatus*), a bottom-feeding fish, living in small schools, often rising and falling in the upper layers of the inshore waters. It is usually between 8 and 16 inches (20–40cm) in length and can weigh up to three pounds (1.4kg). It is easily recognised by its rose-red colouration and two long barbels on the underside of the chin with which it probes the seabed for small worms, crustaceans and molluscs. Because the forked barbels resemble a beard, the fish is known as goatfish and the Greek common name is originally derived from the Venetian *barbon*, meaning beard. The striped red mullet, or surmullet (*Mullus surmuletus*) with a striped dorsal fin, is known as *koutsomoures* and is often mistaken for the more common red mullet.

Both red mullet and the surmullet were much sought after in ancient Greece and in Roman times and became revered as being the tastiest of all fish, so much so that they were depicted in several mosaics in Pompeii. Wealthy Romans are reputed to have constructed seawater ponds in small sheltered bays and fed the fish by hand. There are no records that this procedure was introduced to Corfu by the Venetians, but the fishing by dynamite tale indicates that the small bays and inlets of the coast in the vicinity of Benitses were traditional spawning grounds. Here, the normal type of fishing was by the communal netting method described by Gerry in *Birds, Beasts and Relatives*, when his collecting was again facilitated by Spiro Kokino. A long weighted purse seine net was laid out a few yards offshore and temporarily secured by small boats with several lengths of rope running ashore to stakes in the sand. The net was left in place overnight or for more than one night, and then pulled in to shore in the morning. The fishermen hauled the bulging net on to the sand and began to sort the catch, picking out the various edible fish and sorting each type into a different basket. Gerry made notes on the contents of the various baskets and then turned his attention to the pile of weed, stones and smaller creatures.

Both species, red mullet and surmullet, apparently have a similar taste, especially when pan-fried as *Barbounia tiganita*, for which Lugaretzia had a recipe. Gerry was able to take his pick of the several fish species sorted into baskets on the beach by Spiro Kokino and quite naturally, the rather strange morphology and often bright colour of the *barbounia* was one of his most attractive choices.

## Barbounia Tiganita

Clean, scale and gut 2lbs *barbounia* (3 fish), leaving the heads on; roll in plain flour, lightly salted and peppered and set aside. Sauté two medium-sized sliced onions in ½ cup olive oil in a shallow skillet until tender. Add a clove of chopped garlic, two cups of chopped ripe tomatoes, a sprig of rosemary and a bouquet garni. Transfer to a casserole dish. Slowly bring to the boil, reduce the heat and simmer for ten minutes. Remove bouquet garni, add the fish, cover and simmer for 15–20 minutes. Serve hot.

## *Taki Catches Scorpionfish for Bourbetto*

Gerry was fascinated by the lifestyle of Taki Thanatos from Benitses.

'I have come from Benitses,' he said, 'and I fish on the way. Then I eat and I sleep and when it's night I light my lights and go back to Benitses, fishing again.'

I asked him eagerly what time he intended to start fishing and whether he meant to go round the reefs that lay scattered between the bay and Pondikonissi.

'I start about ten,' he said. 'I work round the island then I head towards Benitses.'

I asked him whether it would be possible for me to join him because, as I explained, there were lots of strange creatures living on the reef which I could not obtain without the aid of a boat.

'Why not?' he said. 'I shall be down below Menelaos'. You come at ten. I'll take you round the reefs and then drop you back at Menelaos before I go to Benitses.'

Gerry ran home excitedly to persuade his mother to let him go night-fishing with Taki and, after he had complied with her wish that he should first have a siesta, she gave him permission to return. When he reached the beach with all his collecting apparel, Taki had already lit the carbide lamp and Gerry could see small fish such as gobies and blennies attracted out of their holes by the light. Taki told him he would row round and round for five minutes so that he could catch whatever there was and then he said he would take him to catch the things he wanted to collect. Suddenly he stopped rowing and pointed to the sandy bottom beneath a submarine cliff. It was a red scorpionfish, Scorpios.

Lying on the sand was a fish, some two feet long with a great filigree of sharp spines, like a dragon's crest along its back, and enormous pectoral fins spread out on the sand. It had a tremendously wide head with golden eyes and a sulky pouting mouth. But it was the colours that astonished me, for it was decked out in a series of reds, ranging from scarlet to wine, pricked out and accentuated here and there with white. It looked immensely sure of itself as it lay there, flamboyant on the sand, and immensely dangerous too. 'This is good eating,' whispered Taki to my surprise, for the fish . . . looked highly poisonous.

Gerry described the way Taki slowly and deliberately lowered the barbed fork of his trident into the water above the fish and then swiftly and neatly drove the five prongs through the back of the fish's great head. Hand over hand, he pulled the pole out of the water and landed the fish on the bottom of the boat, warning Gerry to keep his distance because Scorpios was a bad fish. He managed to lift the fish and drop it into an empty kerosene can, out of harm's way. Taki explained that it was only the spines that were poisonous and that the flesh was as sweet as honey. 'I will give it to you to take home with you,' he said.

Next, he speared an octopus and then, as promised, they headed off towards the island, to land Gerry and his collecting gear on one of the largest flat-topped reefs. Thence, they took Gerry's catch to empty into a rock pool in his favourite bay, and finally back to the jetty below Menelaos'.

Here he strung a cord through the gills of the now dead scorpionfish and handed it to me. 'Tell your mother,' he said, 'to cook it with hot paprika and oil and potatoes and little marrows. It is very sweet.'

Here is a recipe based on Taki's suggestion, given at half past two in the morning when Louisa had begun to convince herself that her son had either drowned or been eaten by a shark. She called the dish Taki's Bourbetto, the Greek name for Scorpionfish Stew, a dish akin to the more familiar French bouillabaisse, of which the Mediterranean red scorpionfish (*Scorpaena scrofa*) is the main ingredient. There is some confusion over the names for fish stew. In Italian it is *brodetto*, in

Corfu it is *bourdetto* (*bourdeto*), while *bourbetto* would seem to be reserved for scorpionfish stew alone.

## Taki's Bourbetto

Gut, clean and wash the fish, taking care to cut off the spines at their bases. In ⅓ pint (or 200 ml) olive oil, sauté 2 finely chopped small onions and 3 minced cloves of garlic. Stir in 1 heaped tablespoon of paprika and a large pinch (or ½ teaspoon) of chilli flakes and fry gently for a few minutes. Add ¾ of a cup of hot water and simmer for ten minutes. Curve the whole fish in the casserole dish, cover with the sauce and then cover with a lid. Stew in the casserole for 40 minutes. Meanwhile, boil small potatoes in their skins and whole small courgettes. Serve the fish in portions with the vegetables on the side and with rough chunks of cornbread to mop up the sauce.

Spiro Kokino and the Communal Fishermen in Gouvia Bay
Waist Deep in the Sea Hauling the Nets

# 11
# A Gourmet Holiday in 1960:
# Still an Idyll

View of Pondikonissi (Mouse Island) from Perama

# A Well-Deserved Break

Gerry wrote to Larry in May 1960 to inform him that he and his wife, Jacquie, planned to take Louisa and Margo back to Corfu for a six-week holiday, the first occasion on which the family had returned to the island since they left in such a hurry in 1939, the first time Jacquie had visited the pastures of her husband's boyhood. The previous six months had been one of the busiest and tiring times of all their lives. Jersey Zoo had opened on 26 March 1959, in time for the influx of Easter Weekend holidaymakers, but Gerry was not present to witness the event. He and Jacquie were away on an expedition in Argentina, from which she returned home in February due to the effects of a head injury sustained in a car crash in Buenos Aires, while he stayed on collecting specimens until June 1959. In the meantime, cleared of any long-term medical problem, she had begun to arrange transfer of animals from Bournemouth to Jersey, as well as designing and decorating the upper floors of Les Augrès Manor – including the creation of a kitchen – for the eventual move of Louisa to live with her son and daughter-in-law in their new home.

New editions of *The Overloaded Ark* and *The Drunken Forest* had appeared on 1 January 1960 and by early May, *A Zoo in*

*My Luggage* was already in press for an October publication date. Between times Gerry had also finished the manuscripts for *Island Zoo* and *Look at Zoos*, and *The Whispering Land*, an account of his Argentinian expedition, was well under way, all three destined to reach the bookshelves during 1961. They were all in need of a break and where better than to return to Corfu, albeit with some anticipation that things may have changed for the worse. In his unpublished autobiography and as an introduction to an article published in the Summer Edition of *Punch* magazine (1961), Gerry wrote:

> There is always, I suppose, an element of risk in returning, after a long absence, to a place in which you were happy, and the risk is, of course, greatly increased if it is a place in which you spent a part of your childhood. You wonder, if you return, whether the place will measure up to your memory of it, or will you find that your memory of it was distorted by the magic eye of childhood. Therefore, when I decided to return for a holiday to the island of Corfu, it was with some trepida-tion, for the journey was obviously going to be fraught with danger. I comforted myself with the thought that Corfu had always been fairly well off the map and must therefore have been by-passed by the tourist trade. I felt sure it would be as I left it.

Gerry viewed the island as still being 'off the beaten track' and the itinerary he planned made it seem even more so than normal. Direct international flights to the island did not begin until April 1965 and the quickest route was on scheduled flights from London to Rome and Rome to Brindisi. According to Jacquie, however, the holiday route Gerry chose was as follows:

> In order to prolong the journey, we decided not to fly from the UK but went to St Malo on the ferry from Jersey. The next day we took the most delightful train to Paris which was a very amusing journey and the staff provided us with a delicious ad hoc lunch which pleased Gerry in particular. After arriving in Paris, we stayed for a few days in the Grand Hotel and met up with some old French friends. The next step of the journey was by train to Rome from where we were forced to fly down to Brindisi to catch the Greek ferry to Corfu.

The final leg of the journey took place on Thursday, 26 May. They were greeted by most unseasonable weather and as they walked up the drive to the house of Michael Chalikiopoulos, son of Spiro, they were hit by an icy wind and a downpour of the largest hailstones Gerry had seen in his life. They started to reminisce above the sound of the hail and were hardly reassured to learn that this summer was proving to be the worst for many years. They spent their first night drinking hot Greek coffee, smiling wryly and no doubt wondering whether this was a welcome of divine retribution. Michael drove them into Corfu Town to find a small pension, leaving them with their request that he might find suitable villa accommodation for their holiday, in much the same way his father had been asked back in 1935.

## *Astakos for Kiroi Durrell*

They stayed the night at a pension in town and, come the grey morning, they decided to remain where there were plenty of places to shelter and where they could watch the sky gradually turn to the expected cloudless blue of their remembrances. The evening remained the same cloudless blue and Gerry enticed Margo to hire a car and drive out west to one of the three bays reputed to be the most beautiful in Corfu, in the village of Paleocastritsa, in search of a typical Corfiot dinner. After all, an essential part of a holiday abroad was to be well and truly catered for as gourmets. As they drove across the island Gerry and Louisa recalled how Spiro had driven the whole family to visit Theo and his wife Mary, daughter Alexia, and Alexia's nanny, in the summer of 1937 when the Stephanides family had rented a small peasant's cottage. There was the embryo of an artist colony in the village to where Larry and Nancy were frequent visitors to meet with the American painter Maurice Koster and the Swiss artist Réné Berlincourt. Theo recalled that, at that time, there were only two hotels in the village, one a private concern, the other run by the government-sponsored Tourist Commission, which ran a daily omnibus to Corfu Town.

To Gerry's delight nothing had changed in 1960. The small hotel still sprawled under the olives with its vine-covered, open-air dining room stretching down to the beach. At the edge of the sea was a sunken wooden cage wherein he could discern live 'choleric looking' lobsters imprisoned. These were not the familiar lobsters of Atlantic Europe with two large claws, but the Mediterranean spiny lobsters which were often referred to as crayfish or *astakos*, as Larry recorded in *Prospero's Cell* – actually, *Palinurus elephas*. They were nocturnal, typical of rocky coasts and usually caught in baited wooden cages, below depths of twenty metres. They were one of Gerry's favourite foods and he dutifully followed the waiter over the slippery rocks to choose one for their meal. The lobster was rubbed generously with sea salt and boiled in a mixture of water and white wine with a single bay leaf. Immersion in boiling water caused the lobster's dowdy natural pigmentation to be denatured a bright red colour. Then, the body would be cut lengthways to expose the white flesh and dressed only with olive oil and lemon juice and perhaps mayonnaise. Often, the oil/lemon juice mix and mayonnaise were served separately in small bowls so that the individual taste of the diner for the delicate flavour of the flesh was not masked. The best restaurants served them thus; others made the flesh spin out further by serving *astako makoronada*, lobster with macaroni sauce.

The hotel proprietor came to the table and enquired if Gerry's name was Durrell and if he was the Kiroi Durrell who had written the book about Corfu. Gerry admitted the fact and the proprietor seemed quite overwhelmed, insisting that he should have a glass of wine for old times' sake. Ever the naturalist and collector, Gerry enquired the best place to catch green lizards, then continued to try out his Greek by asking whether it was the mating season of the octopus, before moving on to discuss the private life of the spiny lobster. These exchanges were punctuated by toasts to each other, their families, his hotel, their holiday and their speedy return to the island the following year. Gerry, who hardly ever drove, noted that he was 'full of wine and feeling very mellow' as Margo took the wheel back to town in the cool dusk, when, 'as if to order, the dark olive groves were suddenly full of the pulsating greenish light of fireflies.'

## Simple Experimental Cuisine at the Annexe

Michael found them somewhere to stay within a couple of days, a small villa, really little more than a recreational beach house known as the Annexe, on the waterfront at Perama, overlooking a half-moon-shaped bay. This was one of Gerry's old stamping grounds and he waxed lyrical.

Here we were soon enveloped in that curious sense of timelessness that is one of the island's chief charms. Soaked in sunshine and food we soon attained the Nirvana where you know that each year has four million days, and each will be as perfect as this one.

Albeit the size of a matchbox, Jacquie remembers the accommodation with fondness.

> Although primitive, the beds were comfortable, and we were looked after by one of Gerry's and Margaret's old school chums, Uranea, who we later christened 'Tyranea' as she was rather overwhelming at times. Cooking facilities were practically nil, so we decided that, apart from a simple breakfast of yoghurts, fruits and tea we would eat out and enjoy the local seafood, whilst we had the chance. The whole point was to give Mother Durrell a complete holiday and rest which she deeply appreciated. Gerry and Margo thoroughly enjoyed meeting their old peasant friends and they spent hours revisiting the old villas and haunts whilst their mother sat in the shade of an olive tree near the water's edge, either knitting or reading.

Although the cooking facilities were generally inadequate, amounting to only a small paraffin stove, both Gerry and his mother were able to indulge themselves in culinary experimentation. Every morning they could hear the shrill cries of an itinerant vendor selling fresh seafood, and each day they tried something different – sea urchins, clams, whitebait, baby cuttlefish, or best of all, red mullet. For Gerry, their preparation was turned into anatomical dissections and examinations, while Louisa was in her element inventing variations of traditional Greek dishes. The edible sea urchin (*Paracentrotus lividus*) is most commonly sought for culinary purposes in the seas between Italy and Greece. The orange gonads of both male and female urchins are commonly used to flavour pasta sauces, but the simplest way to appreciate their delicate taste is to open the urchin's shell from below and remove them with a penknife. They are best enjoyed raw with a squeeze of lemon juice, or as *achinosalata*, a sea urchin salad, drizzled with olive oil, lemon juice and sprinkled with powdered coriander.

The vendor had two types of clams, the common bivalve molluscs of the Venus clam family (*Veneridae*), still to be found on Greek and Italian market stalls. The smooth-shelled clam or brown Venus clam (*Callista chione*) is perhaps more common in fish markets throughout the Mediterranean region. Its Greek name is *gialisteres*, meaning 'shiny' and it is known as *fasolaro* in Italian. The clamshell with rough, raised ridges is most commonly *Venerupis decussata*, called *archiváda* in Greek, *vongole* in Italian, officially in English, the rather cumbersome 'cross-cut carpet shell.' Pasta *archiváda* was quite popular and the kitchen utensils and facilities were sufficiently adequate for Gerry and his mother to follow a simple recipe.

## Pasta Archiváda

Boil 6oz macaroni until al dente in plenty of lightly salted water. Drain and reserve ½ cup pasta water. Heat 3 tbsp olive oil in a skillet and cook 1 chopped garlic clove until golden then add ½ tsp red pepper flakes. Stir in ½ cup of white wine and 2lbs of clams. Cover the skillet and cook for 5–6 minutes until the clams have opened. Remove clams as they open and discard those that remain closed. Add ¼ cup pasta water to the skillet and bring to the boil. Add pasta, toss and cook to soak up liquor. Add the reserved clams with 2 tbsp chopped flat-leaf parsley and toss to mix. Serve and drizzle with a little olive oil.


# Genius Loci Kerkyra

The local landscape and ecology appeared to have changed quite drastically since Gerry was last here, with the airport runway now forming the eastern boundary of Lake Chalikiopoulos and the Second World War causeway linking Kanoni to Perama and altering the hydrology of the inshore marine ecosystem. But Pondikonissi, Mouse Island, was still there, like the upturned remains of Ulysses' boat, as it had ever been alluded to, and the Chessboard Fields, the remains of the Venetian system of salt pans were still visible, albeit a little more unkempt than he remembered. No doubt Old Plop or his heirs and the water snakes would still be frequenting the muddy canals.

The day they arrived there was a *kefalia* (flathead mullet) drive in progress along the western shore of Lake Chalikiopoulos, just like those of yesteryear when Gerry had taken part and returned home with several fish to grill over the charcoal barbecue. Louisa suggested that he tag along again, urging him to see if he could get any roe, so that she might try to make taramasalata in the traditional Venetian/Corfiot style. They were hoping to stay here now for the best part of five weeks and she would have ample time to salt and cure the roe. Gerry duly obliged and his mother quietly began to cure the roe to make the basic *bottarga*, as the cured mullet roes were known in Italian. She left the roes to soak in salted water overnight and sat contentedly with a gin and tonic and her rather unusual selection of books. There was a favourite from the crime fiction genre, *Anatomy of a Murder* by Robert Traver; a new edition of E.M. Forster's *A Passage to India*, chosen to indulge in Indian nostalgia; and of course, the dutiful choice of *Mountolive*, the recently published third volume in Larry's 'Alexandria Quartet'.

Next morning, she wiped and patted the excess moisture from the roes with a kitchen cloth and then rolled them gently in olive oil. Then she carefully tossed them to coat them evenly in coarse sea salt, laying them on a kitchen cloth in a cool dry place to allow the salt to dehydrate the roes. She left them there for about seven days, turning them carefully at regular intervals and replacing the wet cloths with dry ones. After seven days she began to test the hardness of the roes and their suitability for grinding to a rough powder in a mortar and pestle. Louisa's recipe for traditional Venetian/Corfiot *avgotaraho taramasalata*, which she referred to as 'Corfu caviar', was as follows:

## Corfu Caviar

Soak 1oz breadcrumbs and 1oz ground almonds in the
juice of two lemons and 1 cup of water for 15 minutes.
Mix in 4oz finely ground *bottarga* with 1 crushed clove
of garlic and ¼ tsp cayenne pepper. Slowly and gradually
stir in 1 pint of olive oil, ensuring the mixture does not
separate. Serve as a dip with fresh black olives.

These occasions of simple experimental cuisine were, however,
uncommon events. Gerry wrote:

In the evening, sun-drunk, our bodies rough and salty
from the clear waters of the little bay, we would be
unable to face the Herculean task of cooking our own
food, so we would drift down the road to the tiny café
half a mile away. Here, at a table under the mimosa trees,
we would drink our wine and watch the sunset on the
sea, turning it from blue to silver, and then, suddenly,
lighting it up with a blurred peacock iridescence that was
unbelievable.

The café was owned by Menelaos Kondos, a member of the
family with which the Durrells had been close friends in the
1930s. It was called Aegle or Aegli, a popular name meaning
brightness or dazzling light, used for a variety of mythological female characters, notably the brightest of the naiads,

freshwater nymphs of fountains and wells. As the years rolled on, the café became the Aegli Hotel in 1975 and reached its modern majestic form by a rebuild and refurbishment in 1995. It had a reputation as an excellent fish café and restaurant from the early 1950s onwards.

Solo fishermen still plied their trade in the sea below the café in 1960, but the Benitses fishery had been transformed into a communal industry by financial aid provided under the Marshall Aid Program and Mission for the development of the Greek economy, 1947–52. Two large fishing boats were purchased as mother ships of the fleet – *Dimitrios Agios* (Saint Demetrius) painted red, and *Agia Triada* (Holy Trinity) painted grey, the better of the two boats. Every evening it would leave the harbour towing a utility boat, known as a *pisino*, followed by small fire boats (*pyrofania*) with carbide lamps. These scattered to prominent localities to enable their lights to attract fish and when a good shoal had swum within the area marked by these small craft, referred to as *gri gri*, the mother ship would proceed to surround the area with purse seine nets. The nets would be trawled to the beach adjacent to the harbour and the catch selectively sorted.

Red mullet (*barbounia*) was the main target fish along with anchovies (*gavros*) and all the other small silver fish which collectively came to be known as whitebait (*marides*), usually types of smelt and picarel, especially big-scale sand smelt (*Atherina boyeri*). The Aegli specialities were all of these species, fried in a skillet over an open charcoal oven, or barbecue – *barbounia tiganita*, *gavros tiganitos* and *marides tiganites*. Young *soupya* (cuttlefish), boiled and served in a wine sauce was a popular appetizer, as were *garides*, alias the *caramote*, king or striped prawn (*Penaeus kerathurus*), served as *garides saganaki*. Louisa had a recipe for this latter dish, probably collected from the Aegli Café, and she also seems to have possessed a couple of favourite *saganaki*, simply, the skillets which hung in easy reach in all her kitchens.

## Aegli Garides Saganaki

Boil 1lb (500g) raw king prawns in water for five minutes; then drain and set aside to cool. Heat 2 tbsp olive oil in a skillet, add one chopped onion and stir until soft. Mix in 14oz (400g) chopped tomatoes, one clove of minced garlic and simmer for 30 minutes until the sauce has thickened, adding another 1 tbsp oil if required. Dress and peel the cold prawns by pinching off the legs and pulling off the carapace to leave head and tail attached. Stir the dressed prawns into the sauce and simmer for another five minutes. Sprinkle 7oz (200g) of crumbled feta cheese over the mixture, leave to stand and serve as the cheese starts to melt.

The Durrells ate looking across to the seemingly timeless outline of Mouse Island, its shape fretted by dark cypress trees, with its tiny deserted monastery perched on its peak. Then, friends would begin to drift casually through the gloom, wine would continue to flow, and the café and gently rippling waters of the bay would gradually fill with song. During their stay, a big, burnished orange moon rose over the Albanian mountains, waxing through its first quarter to full at two o'clock on the morning of 9 June 1960, then completing its cycle to rise to another full moon on 8 July, the day before they left the island.

Gerry concluded his 1961 article in *Punch* with a most positive paragraph to the effect that he was grateful that he had not been disappointed, and that the essential atmosphere of the island was still the same. He was keen to repeat the greeting that everyone on the island was in the habit of using, which he considered to be the most attractive greeting in the world: 'Be happy.' He was glad to find the island and the islanders were still just that.

Gerry's Favourite Mealtime Memory Cartoon:
Larry and the Surprise Matchbox of Scorpions

# *Afterword by Jacquie Durrell*

*The past is a foreign country, they do things differently there.*
*(L.P. Hartley)*

Yes, times were indeed different; terms like *fast food*, *instant noodles* and *microwaves* had not been invented. Instead great care was taken in the preparation of meals, their ingredients were chosen with imagination and their aroma wakened the curiosity for what was about to be put on the table. David Shimwell has dipped deeply into that past and has meticulously and skilfully unearthed tasty treasures which one might well be tempted to try out at home.

Louisa, my beloved Mother Durrell, desperately wanted to know some of the culinary secrets that were produced by her cooks in India. She had wisely kept the recipes written by her mother and was determined to try them out herself. Although her husband did not want her ever to be involved in domestic matters she had made up her mind to learn how to produce tasty meals and conspired with her cooks to teach her whenever the Master was away on business.

She was a quick learner and meticulously made notes which, unbeknown to her at the time, would eventually come in useful. As it happens, two of her children, Larry and Gerry, took on her mantle and became keen and original cooks in their later years. Reading through Louisa's mother's notes one is immediately transported into a time in the Indian Raj when money was no object, ingredients were readily available and eating meant more than just a quick meal.

But to fast forward by ten years brings us to a time when hunger was often an unwelcome guest and many foods were still rationed and unobtainable. In the years after 1951 after Gerry and I were married, when Mother Durrell had mastered the art of preparing food with whatever was available, she insisted it was time that this lass from the North learnt to enjoy the countless variations of a true Indian curry. I was hooked then and still am.

When Gerry and I took his mother back to Corfu in 1960 it was meant to be a holiday for her, free from the previous culinary demands of the 1930s with which she associated the times spent on the island. She deeply appreciated the holiday, and since our quite simple accommodation provided only a primitive cooker, we unanimously decided to enjoy the local sea food, accompanied by fresh salads and home-grown wines in Greek tavernas.

In this sense, the past in Corfu was truly a foreign country.

**Jacquie Durrell, September 2018**

# Appendix: The Tottering Pile of Cookbooks (and Manuscripts)

Lee Durrell & David Shimwell at Work on the Tottering Pile of Manuscripts (at Les Augrès Manor, 2016)

During the Gerald Durrell Jersey Week in July 2016, I was privileged to study the collection of handwritten manuscripts and printed recipes held in the archives of the Gerald Durrell Story, on display at Les Augrès Manor, Trinity, Jersey, from the collection of Gerry's mother, Mrs Louisa Durrell (1886–1964). This was essentially the 'tottering pile of books' to which Gerry referred in Chapter 2 of *My Family and Other Animals*. It turned out to be an intriguing and eclectic archive. I worked on the archive in the library of the Hostel at Jersey Zoo, either at dusk, with a glass of Gerry's favourite tipple – brandy and soda – to hand, or at dawn with a plate of toast and honey, mindful of one of Gerry's 'zoological breakfasts'. And thus, I recreated two other tottering piles, one comprising published works, which I have called 'Printed Books and Supplements', and a second pile of 'Handwritten Manuscripts', arguably the more interesting pile in that they provide an actual insight into the life of Louisa Durrell and her family.

## Printed Books and Supplements
## (1909–1962)

1909 – *Cassell's Household Cookery* (1909) by Lizzie Heritage, published by Cassell & Company, London, incomplete and lacking a front cover (pages 5–189 only). Page 189 bearing the recipe for Curry Sauce is significantly detached and inserted elsewhere in the text, suggesting frequent reference.

Miss Lizzie Heritage, if that be her given name or a nom de plume, is listed in the *Epicure Directory* as a teacher of cookery and domestic economy with First Class Diplomas in the two subjects from the National Training School, 16 June 1886. The book was first published in 1894 with later editions in 1896, 1901 and 1909. The editions of 1901 and 1909 were honoured with an introduction by Johann Ludwig Wilhelm Thudichum (1829–1901), a German-born medical scientist, pioneer of biomedical research and prolific author of such treatises as 'A Complete Manual of Viticulture and Oenology' and 'On the Coca of Peru and its Immediate Principles'. In the year of her final edition of 1909, Lizzie was resident in the village of Earlsdon, near Coventry in Warwickshire.

1920 – *The Economical Cookery Book (for India)*. Glossary of Hindustani terms with English equivalents. By G.L.R. (1920), published by Thacker, Spink & Co., Calcutta; incomplete and dilapidated (pages 17–252 for recipes 44–695 only).

Thacker, Spink and Co. was a prestigious Kolkata publishing house which was renowned throughout the Indian Raj, first for *Thacker's Bengal Directory* (1864–84), then from 1885 onwards as *Thacker's Indian Directory*. The directory was an almanac and later owned by the Maharaja of Darbhanga, a prominent industrialist, philanthropist and politician after Indian independence.

1926 – *Bengal Sweets* by Mrs J. Haldar (1921) Second Edition (1926). Chuckerverity, Chatterjee & Co. Ltd.

There is an excellent review of this book by Itiriti on the 'Eat to Write and Write to Eat' blog, entitled 'Exploring the Romance of Bengali Sweets with J. Haldar' published online on 14 November 2013. It seems that, like myself, the reviewer did not know her forename either. 'Haldar' is a prominent Bengali surname, based in Calcutta.

1936 – *500 Cookery Dishes That You Can Make For Sixpence Each* by Mary Woodham (1936) published by E. Foulsham & Company, London. Incomplete, dilapidated and foxed (pages 35–158 only).

The Foulsham Company was noted as being the publisher of *Raphael's Almanac*, annually on 1 August, apparently every year since 1819. There is an advert for the almanac on the last page of the above cookery book, to indicate that it discussed topics which Louisa would have read avidly in connection with her special interest in folklore, heritage, the supernatural and fortune telling; such subjects as: 'The voice of the Heavens and a Weather Guide for each month'; 'General Predictions'; 'A Domestic Guide: when to Bake, Brew, Hire Servants, Set Fowls'; 'Birthday Information and the Fate of any Child for every day of the year'.

Two complete books, now on the kitchen shelves at Les Augrès Manor, were probably birthday presents from Gerry to his mother:

1954 – *Indian Cooking* by Savitri Chowdhary (1954) Andre Deutsch, London.

This book was a most appropriate choice for his mother because the author was born in Multan, Punjab and made her home in England from 1932 onwards, after following her husband who had studied medicine and then went on to work in a practice in Laindon, Essex. She immersed herself in English life, but remained in touch with her Indian self, publishing one of the earliest Indian cookery books and making numerous television appearances to demonstrate her skills. She had also been involved in the Celebration of Indian Independence in the Albert Hall in 1947. In her memoir, *I Made My Home in England*, she recounts her experiences of migration and settlement in England in the 1930s. She is a topic in a current Open University programme.

1957 – *Best Food from India* by RAP Hare OBE (1957) Arco Publications Limited, London.

*c.*1950s–1962 – Printed supplements from magazines to 1962, with such titles as 'Cooking with Robert Carrier'; 'Ways with Custard' from *Woman* magazine by editor Ruth Morgan; 'Round Britain Cookery', five supplement booklets from the Good Housekeeping Institute, including 'International Kitchen' and 'Oriental Cookery'.

## Handwritten Manuscripts
### (1887–*c.*1940)

1887 – Copperplate handwritten recipes from a manuscript dated 1887. Contents page: Milk Punch; Common Seed Cake; Fritters; Tap Sauce; Breakfast Cake; Soda Cake; Sponge Biscuits; Ginger Cake; Yorkshire Pudding; Madira [*sic*] Cake; Almond Cakes; German Puffs; Scones; Geneva Pasties; Sponge Cake; Mango Chutnee; Tomato Sauce; Cheese Pudding; Jew Pickle; Toffy [*sic*]; Sweet Chutnee; A Cake; Apricot Cheese; Chappatis

1920s – Thin Octavo hardback notebook on display at The Gerald Durrell Story, Jersey Zoo; usually open at the bespattered and foxed pages for the Tomato Ketchup and Plum Cake (Indian) recipes, though the page is turned from time to time to prevent deterioration on constant exposure to light. There is also a recipe for Bengal Chicken Curry, which is essentially the same as Gerry's Favourite Curry, of which there are many handwritten and typescript copies in both Jersey and Corfu.

*c.*1923 – Quarto hardback notebook of Dulwich College with handwritten recipes from the time Larry and Leslie were in school in England and their parents travelled between India and England. Sweet Mango Chutney or Apples; Plum Cake; Plum Pudding; Indian Budgees; Dropped Scones; Ginger Wine; Strawberry Foam; Whey Pudding; Lavender Cake; Lemon Blancmange; Lemon Syrup; Bread; Tamarind Chutnee; Loquat Pickle; Salad Dressing; Plum Pudding (Indian Way); Indian Fudge Chocolate; Onions 'Goodenough'; Macaroni Cheese; Eggs a la St James; Baked Rhubarb Pudding; Apples & Marrow Chutney; Lemon Balm Pudding; Marmalade; Chocolate Pudding; Kirk Pudding. Rather perversely, there is also a recipe for Floor Polish and a knitting pattern for a Sleeveless Pullover.

The notebook would probably have originated from the time when Leslie Durrell (aged 6) and brother Larry (11) lived at 36 Hillsborough Road which backed on to Dulwich College, in 1923. Leslie entered Dulwich College in 1923, where he apparently spent an unhappy and unsuccessful three years and the notebook is clearly a relic of this time. In 1926, their father, Lawrence Samuel Durrell, bought a house at 43 Alleyn Park, Dulwich and there are references to the property in the proceedings of the Dulwich Society. The family lived there until 1928. It contains both Indian and British recipes.

*c.*1930–1940 – Leather-bound, loose-leaf folder with miscellaneous handwritten recipes and knitting patterns – ostensibly Bournemouth and the Corfu years.

Handwritten recipes: Light Layer Cake; Honey Cake; Cake without Eggs; Walnut Cake; Queen Pudding; Coconut Pudding; Anchovy Salad; Cheese Beignets; Apple Mousse; Coconut Biscuits; Almond Cheese; a Salt Cod Casserole (Gk); Kokkinisto; Corfu Fish Stew; Cream of Apples; French Pancakes; Shrimp Soufflé; Indian Fudge Chocolate; Walnut Fudge; Peppermint Sweets; Rich Puff Pastry; Short Crust; Tomatoes Stuffed; Tomato Tart; Vegetable Marrow Cakes; Tomatoes Indian.

The handwritten knitting patterns include those for a Sleeveless Pullover – of the type worn by Gerry as a boy in Corfu – and a Fisherman's Cap of the type favoured by Larry and depicted on his bust in the 'Bosketto Durrell', the most prominent municipal gardens in Corfu Town. Other patterns include a Roll-Neck Raglan Sweater; Cable-Stitch Raglan Cardigan; Cap-Sleeve Jumper and Spiral Socks.

David Shimwell

Les Augrès, Jersey, August 2018

# *Acknowledgements*

Throughout my compilation of the manuscript Lee Durrell has been a constant adviser, facilitator and friend. I will ever be grateful for her help and guidance and for her grant of permission to use quotations from the vast literary resources of the Estate of Gerald Durrell. She also granted open access to the culinary archive of Louisa Durrell. I am also grateful to the following friends: Anne Binney for provoking and masterminding 'The Gerald Durrell Story' exhibition at Les Augrès, Jersey; Jacquie Durrell for lively discussions and a postludium; Alexina and David Ashcroft, respectively former Administrative Assistant and Director of the Durrell School of Corfu, latterly, facilitators of the annual Gerald Durrell Corfu Week, and whencesoever, for unbounded friendship; Sarah Drury, former Director of the Durrell School of Corfu, for kindness and for field and market research; Colin Stevenson for nonpareil photography, fresh vegetables and many a nippitaty; Theo Quant, godson of Theodore Stephanides, for stimulating discussions on the philosophies of Heraclitus; Peter Sutton for his encyclopedic knowledge of the fauna of Corfu and for companionship; Paul Walden, Durrell Wildlife Trust, Life Member, for nudging elbows and for general support; Malcolm Campbell for research assistance; Sarah Atkinson for constant inspiration and support; and finally, to Rosemary and Dave Bellamy whose kind invitation initiated my long-lasting Durrell association.

My agent, Norah Perkins, of Curtis Brown provided astute negotiation with commissioning editor, Maddy Price, of Hodder & Stoughton, whose vision initiated the project. Rupert Lancaster, Non-Fiction Publisher, and Cameron Myers carried the baton further.

# Text Permissions

The author wishes to thank the following for permission to quote from copyrighted works. Every attempt has been made to contact the copyright holders, however, if any omissions have occurred please contact the publishers and we will rectify any errors at the earliest opportunity.

Permission for the use of quotations from Gerald Durrell's works is kindly granted by Curtis Brown Group Ltd on behalf of the Estate of Gerald Durrell.

Permission for the use of quotations from Lawrence Durrell's works is kindly granted by Curtis Brown Group Ltd on behalf of the Estate of Lawrence Durrell.

Copyright © Joanna Hodgkin 2012, reproduced by permission of Virago, an imprint of Little, Brown Book Group Ltd

Copyright © Henry Miller 1941, reproduced by permission of the Estate of Henry Miller, courtesy of The Curtis Brown Group Ltd.

# Sources and Notes

The main sources for the contextual extracts are the three books by Gerald Durrell published in a single volume *The Corfu Trilogy* (2006) by Penguin Books. The three books published separately are as follows:

Gerald Durrell (1956). *My Family and Other Animals.* Rupert Hart-Davis.

Gerald Durrell (1969). *Birds, Beasts and Relatives.* William Collins Sons & Co Ltd.

Gerald Durrell (1978). *The Garden of the Gods.* William Collins Sons & Co Ltd.

Two other publications are also of major importance:

Lawrence Durrell (1945). *Prospero's Cell. A guide to the landscape and manners of the island of Corfu.* Faber & Faber.

Theodore Stephanides (2011). *Autumn Gleanings. Corfu Memoirs & Poems.* The Durrell School of Corfu.

Each chapter has a sequential list of appropriate references to these and other sources.

### Chapter 1. An Indian Culinary Heritage:
### Louisa Dixie-Durrell and her Cuisine

1 There are several published accounts of the history of the Durrell and Dixie families in the various biographies of both Lawrence and Gerald Durrell, each with subtle variations. The account in this chapter is derived primarily from the unpublished *Autobiographical Fragments*, a typescript compiled by Gerald Durrell, lodged in the archives at Les Augrès Manor, Jersey. The recent book by Michael Haag *The Durrells of Corfu* (2017) Profile Books, London, includes an accurate illustrated account of the time spent by the family in the Greek island of Corfu.

2 Gerald Durrell (1956). *My Family and Other Animals, Chapter 2 The Strawberry-Pink Villa*.

3 Gerald Durrell (1956). *My Family and Other Animals, The Migration*.

4 Gerald Durrell (1978). *The Garden of the Gods, Chapter 6 The Royal Occasion*.

5 Gerald Durrell (1978). *The Garden of the Gods, Chapter 8 The Merriment of Friendship*.

6 Gerald Durrell (1978). *The Garden of the Gods, Chapter 5 Fakirs and Fiestas*.

7 Gerald Durrell (1978). *The Garden of the Gods, Chapter 8 The Merriment of Friendship*.

8 www.tata.com/company/profileinside/Jamshedpur-Utilities-and-Services-Company.

9 *The Economical Cookery Book (for India). A thoroughly practical manual of simple and dainty dishes connected with the correct method of serving them . . . French culinary terms and a Glossary of Hindustani terms with English equivalents (1920).*

10 Mrs J. Haldar (1921). *Bengal Sweets* (Second Edition 1926). Chuckerverity, Chatterjee & Co., Ltd. Booksellers and Publishers.

## Chapter 2. Heritage Recipes from the Empire of Queen Victoria

1 All the recipes herein referred to are listed in the Appendix to this book, *The Tottering Pile of Cookbooks and Manuscripts*. Other text references are as follow

2 https://en.wikipedia.org/wiki/Golden_Jubilee_of_Queen_Victoria

3 Joanna Hodgkin (2013). *Amateurs in Eden, Chapter 6 Prospero's Island* (page 170).

4 Gerald Durrell (1978). *The Garden of the Gods, Chapter 5 Fakirs and Fiestas.*

5 Gerald Durrell (1956). *My Family and Other Animals, Chapter 9 The World in a Wall.*

6 Gerald Durrell (1956). *My Family and Other Animals, Chapter 14 The Talking Flowers.*

### Chapter 3. Curries in Context

1 Theodore Stephanides (2011). *Autumn Gleanings; At the Villa Anemoyanni* (pages 55-56).

2 Gerald Durrell (1956). *My Family and Other Animals, Chapter 6 The Sweet Spring.*

3 Lawrence Durrell (1935). *Pied Piper of Lovers; Book 1, Chapter 1.*

4 Gerald Durrell (1978). *The Garden of the Gods, Chapter 4 The Elements of Spring.*

5 Lawrence Durrell (1945). *Prospero's Cell, Chapter X Lear's Corfu.*

6 Edward Lear (2015). *Birds Drawn for Sir John Gould, 1832–1838.* Folio Society.

7 Edward Lear (1871, 2009). *Nonsense Songs, Stories, Botany, and Alphabets.* British Library Publishing Division.

8 Mary Woodman (1935). *500 Cookery Dishes That You Can Make For 6$^D$ Each.* W. Foulsham & Co., Ltd. London.

9 Currency crisis and collapse in interwar Greece. eprints. lse.ac.uk/44881/GreeSE%20No60.pdf.

### Chapter 4. Savoury Finger Foods and Palate-Pleasers

1 Gerald Durrell (1978). *The Garden of the Gods, Chapter 8 The Merriment of Friendship.*

2 https://en.wikipedia.org/wiki/Kasseri. https://en. wikipedia.org/wiki/Sirene

3 Gerald Durrell (1971). *Fillets of Plaice, Chapter 1 The Birthday Party.*

4 Theodore Stephanides (2011). *Autumn Gleanings: Ionian Banquets* (page 35).

5 David Shimwell (2012). The nature of horta or Greek greens. https://www.creativecowboyfilms.com/blog_posts/the-nature-of-horta-or-greek-greens

## Chapter 5. A Culinary Heritage of the Durrell Family in Corfu

1 Anna Lillios (2004) (ed.) *Lawrence Durrell and the Greek World* (page 36): Susan & Ian MacNiven, *Margaret Durrell Remembers: A Dialogue in Corfu* 2000. Associated Universities Presses.

2 Theodore Stephanides (2011). *Autumn Gleanings; First Meeting with Lawrence Durrell,* (pages 25–34). Durrell School of Corfu.

3 Gerald Durrell (1969). *Birds, Beasts and Relatives, Part III, The Olive Merry-Go-Round.*

4 Gerald Durrell (1978). *The Garden of the Gods, Chapter 6 The Royal Occasion.*

5 Gerald & Lee Durrell (1982). *The Amateur Naturalist, Chapter One The Naturalist on Home Ground.* Book Club Associates/Hamish Hamilton.

6  Factsheet Rice https://ec.europa.en/agriculture/sites/ agriculture/files/cereals/factsheet-rice-2_en.pdf

7  Colonel A.R. Kenney-Herbert (1879). *Culinary Jottings from Madras: a treatise in thirty chapters on reformed cookery for Anglo-Indian exiles.* (2016 and 2018 reprints available)

8  https://en.wikipedia.org/wiki/Arthur_Robert_Kenney-Herbert

9  Gerald Durrell (1956). *My Family and Other Animals, Chapter 3 The Rose-Beetle Man..*

10  Gerald Durrell (1991). *Marrying Off Mother* and other stories: *Marrying Off Mother,* (pages 60-90).

## Chapter 6. The Influence of Theodore Stephanides

1  Theodore Stephanides (2011). *Autumn Gleanings; First Meeting with Lawrence Durrell,* (pages 25-34). Durrell School of Corfu.

2  Gerald Durrell (1978). *The Garden of the Gods, Chapter 2 Ghosts and Spiders.*

3  Anthony Berkeley Cox  https://en.wikipedia.org/wiki/ Anthony_Berkeley_Cox

4  John Davy (1842). *Notes and Observations on the Ionian Islands and Malta. 2 volumes.* Smith, Elder & Company, London.

5  Lawrence Durrell (1945). *Prospero's Cell, Chapter VI Landscape with Olive Trees 15.1.38.*

6  Henry Miller (1941). *The Colossus of Maroussi: Part One*, (page 17).

7  Theodore Stephanides (2011). *Autumn Gleanings; Kalami Again* (page 60).

8  Gerald Durrell (1956). *My Family and Other Animals*, *Chapter 15 The Cyclamen Woods*.

9  Erotokritos  https://en.wikipedia.org/wiki/ Erotokritos

10  Lawrence Durrell (1945). *Prospero's Cell, Chapter IX Appendix for Travellers, Drinks To Try.*

11  Theodore Stephanides (1973). *Island Trails*. Macdonald and Company, London.

12  Joanna Hodgkin (2013). *Amateurs in Eden, Chapter 6 Prospero's Island* (page 167).

13  Gerald Durrell (1956). *My Family and Other Animals*, *Chapter 6 The Sweet Spring.*

14  Theodore Stephanides (1951). *The microscope and the practical principles of observation.* Faber & Faber.

## Chapter 7. The Delights of Afternoon Tea

1  Gerald Durrell (1978). *The Garden of the Gods, Chapter 8 The Merriment of Friendship.*

2  Gerald Durrell (1969). *Birds, Beasts and Relatives, Part III The Angry Barrells.*

3  Gerald Durrell (1978). *The Garden of the Gods, Chapter 1 Dogs, Dormice and Disorder.*

4 Mrs J. Haldar (1921). *Bengal Sweets* (Second Edition 1926). Chuckerverity, Chatterjee & Co., Ltd. Booksellers and Publishers.

5 Gerald Durrell (1956). *My Family and Other Animals, Chapter 6 The Sweet Spring.*

6 Gerald Durrell (1978). *The Garden of the Gods, Chapter 4 The Elements of Spring.*

7 Joanna Hodgkin (2013). *Amateurs in Eden, Chapter 6 Prospero's Island* (page 167).

8 Lawrence Durrell (1945). *Prospero's Cell, Chapter V History and Conjecture 16.11.37.*

## Chapter 8. Cooking for Larry's International Guests

1 Theodore Stephanides (2011). *Autumn Gleanings. At the Villa Anemoyanni (pages 55–6).*

2 Gerald Durrell (1956). *My Family and Other Animals, Part Two, Chapter 8 The Tortoise Hills.*

3 Gerald Durrell (1969). *Birds, Beasts and Relatives, Part III The Pygmy Jungle.*

4 Magnus Nilsson (2015). *The Nordic Cook Book.* Phaidon Press Limited, London and New York.

5 Gerald Durrell (1978). *The Garden of the Gods, Chapter 2 Ghosts and Spiders.*

6 Gerald Durrell (1978). *The Garden of the Gods, Chapter 3 The Garden of the Gods.*

## Chapter 9. Cooking the Catch
## and Roasting the Bag

1 Lawrence Durrell (1945). *Prospero's Cell, Chapter I Divisions Upon Greek Ground, 29.4.37.*

2 Theodore Stephanides (2011). *Autumn Gleanings: Lawrence Durrell and Nature,* (pages 43–4).

3 Lawrence Durrell (1945). *Prospero's Cell, Chapter IX Appendix for Travellers, Dishes to Experiment With.*

4 Joanna Hodgkin (2012). *Amateurs in Eden, Chapter 6 Prospero's Island* (page 173).

5 Gerald Durrell (1956). *My Family and Other Animals, Part One, Chapter 6 The Sweet Spring.*

6 Theodore Stephanides (2011). *Autumn Gleanings. Lawrence Durrell and Nature* (page 45).

7 Lawrence Durrell (1945). *Prospero's Cell, Chapter III Ionian Profiles, 7.8.37*

8 Lawrence Durrell (1945). *Prospero's Cell, Chapter IX Appendix for Travellers, For Hunters.*

9 Gerald Durrell (1956). *My Family and Other Animals, Chapters 6 The Sweet Spring; 12 The Woodcock Winter; 16 The Lake of the Lilies.*

10 Gerald Durrell (1978). *The Garden of the Gods, Chapter 8 The Merriment of Friendship.*

11 Gerald Durrell (1969). *Birds, Beasts and Relatives, Part III Owls and Aristocracy.*

## Chapter 10. Gerry's Hunter–Gatherer Contributions

1 Gerald Durrell (1969). *Birds, Beasts and Relatives, Part II Perama, The Bay of the Olives.*

2 Gerald Durrell (1956). *My Family and Other Animals, Part Three, Chapter 17 The Chessboard Fields.*

3 Gerald Durrell (1978). *The Garden of the Gods, Chapter 8 The Merriment of Friendship.*

4 Culture-Based Fisheries: Valliculture. www.fao.org/docrep/t8598e/t8598206.htm

5 Gerry's 'Home-Range' as a Hunter-Gatherer is now the area designated as Paraktia Thalassia Zoni Apo Kanoni Eos Mesongi (the Inshore Marine Ecosystem from Kanoni to Mesongi): A European Community Special Protection Area (SPA) and Special Area of Conservation SAC), Code GR2230005, as defined by **Natura** 2000 http://natura2000.eea.europa.eu/natura2000/SDF.aspx-?site=GR2230005

6 Gerald Durrell (1991). *Marrying off Mother and other stories, Marrying off Mother*, pages 60-90.

## Chapter 11. A Gourmet Holiday in 1960: Still an Idyll

1 Gerald Durrell (1961). Summer in Corfu. *Summer Punch*, No. 6296. May 17, 746-8. [Companion to this

article is 'Summer in England' on pages 751-3 of the
same magazine, by Dame Rebecca West (1892–1983),
internationally well-known author and journalist.]

2  Correspondence between the author and Jacquie
Durrell, August–September 2018.

3  Menelaos (Kondos) is mentioned in Gerald Durrell
(1969). *Birds, Beasts and Relatives, Part II Perama, The
Bay of the Olives.* [see also *Dining with the Durrells*,
Chapter 10 (iv).

4  https://en.wikipedia.org/wiki/Corfu_International_
Airport History of Corfu International Airport

5  discovery.ucl.sc.uk/1217677/ The economic dimensions
of the Marshall Plan in Greece 1947-1952.

6  https://atcorfu.com/benitses-photos-1950-celebrities
Benitses 1950s

# A MESSAGE FROM DURRELL WILDLIFE CONSERVATION TRUST

Gerald Durrell's childhood efforts at zoo-keeping, which so bemused his long-suffering family, were the beginning of a lifelong dedication to saving endangered species. What he learned on Corfu from mentors such as Theo inspired his crusade to preserve the rich diversity of animal life on our planet.

This crusade to preserve endangered species did not end with Gerald Durrell's death in 1995. His work goes on through the untiring efforts of Durrell Wildlife Conservation Trust.

Over the years many readers of Gerald Durrell's books have been so motivated by his experiences and vision that they have wanted to continue the story for themselves by supporting the work of his Trust. We hope that you will feel the same way today because through his books and life, Gerald Durrell set us all a challenge. 'Animals are the great voteless and voiceless majority,' he wrote, 'who can only survive with our help'.

Please don't let your interest in conservation end when you turn this page. Visit our website to find out how you can be part of our crusade to save animals from extinction.

For further information, or to send a donation, write to

Durrell Wildlife Conservation Trust

Les Augrès Manor
Jersey, Channel Islands, JE3 5BP
UK

Website: www.durrell.org
Email: info@durrell.org

# An invitation from the publisher

Join us at www.hodder.co.uk, or follow us
on Twitter @hodderbooks to be a part of
our community of people who love the very
best in books and reading.

Whether you want to discover more about a book
or an author, watch trailers and interviews, have the
chance to win early limited editions, or simply browse
our expert readers' selection of the very best books,
we think you'll find what you're looking for.

And if you don't, that's the place to tell us what's missing.

**We love what we do, and we'd love you to be a part of it.**

www.hodder.co.uk

@hodderbooks

HodderBooks

HodderBooks